Cheering for Christ Always

101 Devotions

for

CHRISTIAN CHEERLEADERS OF AMERICA

Through Jesus, therefore, let us continually offer to God a sacrifice of praise - the fruit of lips that confess his name.
Hebrews 13:15

by

Marilyn Phillips

and

Rebekah Phillips

Contact Information

Christian Cheerleaders of America
P.O. Box 49
Bethania, NC 27010

Phone number
1.877.CHEERCCA (243.3722)

Fax Number 866.222.1093

General Information
info@cheercca.com

Visit www.mphillipsauthor.com for more
information about Marilyn Phillips and Rebekah Phillips.

Acknowledgments

Special thanks to Nolan Phillips (Marilyn's husband and Rebekah's father) for editing and formatting this book. Nolan has taught adult Bible studies for over 40 years and was our advisor on this project. We couldn't have done it without him!

Christian Cheerleaders of America

Building PEOPLE before Pyramids

Christian Cheerleaders of America began in 1987 by teaching camps in a few areas with only a small staff of high school and college cheerleaders. Immediately, requests poured in to extend camps to areas across America.

CCA offers "state of the art" cheerleading techniques, materials and methods, while maintaining Christian standards. CCA promotes and encourages academic excellence from cheerleaders. Staff members develop, advise and educate cheerleaders and cheerleader coaches on safety guidelines and techniques.

Outstanding achievers both individually, and as teams, are rewarded and recognized at CCA competitions. Creativity and enthusiasm with a "be the best that you can be" attitude is continually encouraged and promoted.

CCA, above all, gives our Lord Jesus Christ pre-eminence in all we do. This is why we are known for ...

Building PEOPLE before Pyramids!

1 ✝ CREATED BY GOD

For you created my inmost being; you knit me together in my mother's womb.
Psalms 139:13

Isn't it fun to celebrate your birthday! Did you know that your birthday was planned by God long before it actually occurred? Not only that, but also God created a unique "you" to do specific ministry? The talents and gifts He gave you prepare you to minister to others in your life. Our daily decisions influence the people God puts in our lives. We were created by God for a purpose – to glorify Him in all we do. Seek to honor God daily through your words and actions. Do you visualize yourself as God's child before you speak or act? How will this influence what you say or do?

Instructions for Praises and Prayers
The spaces below are for you to record your praises and prayers each day. Enter the date of your specific prayers. When God answers, go back and write that date and how He provided. You will be amazed to see how God intervenes in your life.

Praises and Prayers

_____

_____

_____

_____

2 ✟ SIN

For all have sinned and fall short of the glory of God.
Romans 3:23

What is sin? It is any thought or action that separates us from God. In fact, Habakkuk 1:13 states that God's *eyes are too pure to look on evil …* So to stay in fellowship with God, we must learn to recognize sin in our lives? Basically, sin is doing things our way instead of God's way. The first step to understanding sin is knowing what the Bible says about it. God laid out His basic principles of life in the Ten Commandments. Do you know where to find the Ten Commandments in the Bible? They are found in Exodus 20:1-17. Jesus made the commandments even stricter when He said it was sin when we even think about violating them. Jesus also summarized them into two basic principles: love God, and love others as yourself. God provided His commandments to show how to live a full life that honors Him. Each of us fail to keep the commandments, so it was necessary for God to provide another way. Jesus paid the penalty for our sin that we might live through Him. Do you understand your personal need for a Savior?

Praises and Prayers

_____

_____

_____

_____

3 ✞ FORGIVENESS

As far as the east is from the west, so far has he removed our transgressions from us.
Psalms 103:12

Eternity is real, and we all will live forever. However, our destination in eternity is a choice. We can believe in God, trust in His provision for covering our sin, and spend eternity in heaven, or refuse to believe, reject His provision, and let our destination be eternal separation from God. Sin separates us from God. We all have sinned. God gives us the promise that our sins will be forgiven and forgotten. When you confess your sins and trust in His provision, God forgives. Jesus died on the cross to pay for every sin that we committed in the past and every sin that we will commit in the future. We sin daily. You might be thinking that your sins aren't as bad as others. For instance, you have never murdered anyone. But in God's eyes, all sins are transgressions of His Law. Jesus said that you are guilty of all sin if you are guilty of any. Have you trusted in Jesus as God's provision for your sin?

Praises and Prayers

_____

_____

_____

_____

4 ✟ GOD'S GRACE

For it is by grace you have been saved, through faith - and this not from yourselves, it is the gift of God, not by works, so that no one can boast.
Ephesians 2:8-9

Is there anything that we can do to earn salvation? No, nothing. Earning salvation is like trying to swim from Los Angeles to Hawaii. An Olympic swimmer might make it much further than we could, but we all fail to reach the goal of arriving on the shores of Hawaii. Salvation is a gift from God that came at a great price, the death of Jesus Christ. Salvation is yours if you have been saved. You can't be good enough to earn salvation – remember, if you are guilty of one sin, you are guilty of all. The classic example of this is the answer to the question, "How many rotten eggs does it take to spoil the whole omelet?" Well, just one bad egg is enough! It's the same principle with sin. There isn't anything that you can do to deserve salvation – the requirement is absolute perfection. It is a Gift from God. He offers us the perfection of Jesus in exchange for all of our failures. Pretty good deal! Have you received the gift of salvation?

Praises and Prayers

_____

_____

_____

_____

The Day I was Saved

You better shape up!" my best friend said.
OH! I'm so crushed! Thoughts race through my head!
How could she think my holier than thou attitude was bad?
It's ok if I tell her my husband made me mad.
He didn't want to go to church that night,
I just didn't think that was right!
On the way home from church filled with such hurt I cry.
Little did I know, God was leading me to take the plank out of my eye.
My uncontrollable crying forced me to stop in the parking lot.
That was where God got my attention – my life was finally bought.
When I was ten, I said I believed in Jesus and was baptized.
All this time I had not realized that I was not saved!
The sin in my life had me enslaved.
At ten, what was repentance and sin?
I don't kill, steal, or lie was my thinking within.
On church attendance, and works I could no longer rely.
My life couldn't be bought no matter how hard I tried.
I studied the Bible, searched, listened, and learned
And did not know something was left unearned.
I never earned the right to know God as my savior,
Did not know that complete surrender was the behavior.
This was a divine appointment, I have no doubt!
From that tomb of sin I was about to break out!
God knew about that moment before I was born,
I surrendered and said, "I can't do this without You." And was reborn!
I said, "I am so sorry, please forgive me for my sins."
"Guide me – Jesus, be the Lord of my life."
This is where my new life begins.
The complete surrender feels good.
God's words in the Bible are now understood.
Even though new life begins, This doesn't mean I never sin,
But with the Holy Spirit within, I won't be ignorant of my sins.
When I ask God for forgiveness and turn away,
The Holy Spirit convicts and I want to obey.
This is my story about God leading me to salvation,
I can't wait to hear about your revelation.

© Beth Perry . Used by permission.

5 ✟ ACTION

For we are God's workmanship, created in Christ Jesus to do good works, which God prepared in advance for us to do.
Ephesians 2:10

We often wonder what God has planned for us. Much energy is focused on which college to attend or which profession to choose. Perhaps focusing on God's plan for today is just as important as the future. We tend to think that today's activities do not affect the future. However, God has prepared works for us to do each day, and God has equipped us with everything we need to accomplish His will. The Biblical principle is: the person who is faithful in small things will be rewarded with greater responsibility (see Luke 19:17). Are you faithful in the small things God calls you to do? What is God calling you to do today that will minister to others and point them to God?

Praises and Prayers

_____

_____

_____

_____

6 ✟ CHILDLIKE FAITH

People were bringing little children to Jesus to have him touch them, but the disciples rebuked them. When Jesus saw this, he was indignant. He said to them, "Let the little children come to me, and do not hinder them, for the kingdom of God belongs to such as these. I tell you the truth, anyone who will not receive the kingdom of God like a little child will never enter it." And he took the children in his arms, put his hands on them and blessed them.

Mark 10:13-16

"I became a Christian at an early age. I decided I was ready to be baptized when I was nine. My life has changed in many ways since becoming a Christian. I attend church and really understand the lessons. I help out with the preschool kids at my church on Wednesday nights. I feel like I have The Shepherd leading me in the right direction."

by Harley

Your age doesn't matter. You have to come to that same point that Harley did where you surrender to the Lordship of Jesus and follow Him. Has this happened to you? Share your life changing event with someone.

Praises and Prayers

_____

_____

_____

_____

7 ♱ QUIET TIME WITH GOD

For God is not a God of disorder but of peace.
1 Corinthians 14:33a

Life is stressful. It's difficult to handle homework, friends, family, and cheerleading. Sometimes we are distracted and just don't feel peace every day. God is a God of peace. How do you get the peace that God offers? God's peace only comes through a relationship with Him. We must spend time with Him each day. Do you have a quiet time when you can read the Bible and pray? Remember, praying is just talking to God and listening for His response. Many times, I find that His response comes to me as the Holy Spirit speaks to me while I am reading His Word. Try keeping a notebook by your Bible so you can write down the Scriptures that God uses to touch your heart. Did you have a quiet time with God today? Or, perhaps you don't even know how to have a quiet time. It is really simple. Find a place and time when you won't be interrupted (no TV, radio, loud music or other distractions). Focus on getting quiet before God. Read a selection from Scripture. Visualize what the Bible is telling you. Pray (just talk to God as you would a friend) and then, most important, listen!

by Marilyn

Praises and Prayers

_____

_____

_____

_____

8 ♱ GUARD YOUR HEART

And the peace of God, which transcends all understanding, will guard your hearts and your minds in Christ Jesus.
Philippians 4:7

Scripture challenges us to *"guard your hearts and minds in Christ Jesus."* How can you do that? Do you limit the things you watch on TV? What kind of movies do you watch? Is the music you listen to uplifting God's message to your heart? What kind of books do you read? Are you wasting your time, or are you choosing music, TV shows, books, and movies that will be worthy of your time? The Bible says what we see affects us. *Your eye is the lamp of your body. When your eyes are good, your whole body also is full of light. But when they are bad, your body also is full of darkness* (Luke 11:34). The way to peace is to guard your heart and keep your mind focused on Jesus. How did you guard your heart today?

Praises and Prayers

_____

_____

_____

_____

9 ✞ PROTECTION

See, I have engraved you on the palms of my [God's] hands; your walls are ever before me.
Isaiah 49:16

I have an engraved silver frame from one of the cheerleading teams that I coached. The engraved message reminds me of the team members. The words are etched into the frame and cannot be removed. Scripture says that you are engraved on the palms of God's hands. The second thought is that God will not remove His eyes from us. The walls represent the walls of Jerusalem and by comparison, our lives, but Jesus said, *And surely I am with you always, to the very end of the age.* (Matthew 28:20b) What does that mean do you? I think it means that for the rest of your life you will not be removed from the power of God's hands or from His watchful eye. Does this make a difference to you?

by Marilyn

Praises and Prayers

_____

_____

_____

_____

10 ✝ GOD'S POWER

Now to him who is able to do immeasurably more than all we ask or imagine, according to his power that is at work within us.
Ephesians 3:20

Are there times in your life where you are overwhelmed with God's power at work within you? Has God answered a prayer in a way that can only be explained by, "It's God's power?" There was a time when I had to have radiation five times a week for six weeks due to breast cancer. I was in a large room where the radiation was aimed directly at the cancer site. The technician would step out of the room as the radiation was administered. As I lay on the table I felt hopeless and alone, so I prayed. Instantly, I felt God's presence and knew God would give me the strength and courage to endure radiation treatments. Has God given you power to succeed in a situation when you couldn't imagine success without Him? Did you feel his power at work within you? What does this experience tell you about the things that you are facing today?

by Marilyn

Praises and Prayers

_____

_____

_____

_____

11 ✟ PEACE

May the God of hope fill you with all joy and peace as you trust in him, so that you may overflow with hope by the power of the Holy Spirit.
Romans 15:13

Have you ever been in a situation where you felt hopeless? Not long ago, my daughter was in the hospital and due to an adverse reaction of two antibiotic drugs, her kidneys began to fail. I felt hopeless as the kidney functions decreased daily. Many were praying for Rebekah. In prayer, I gave the situation to God, and an amazing peace came! My daughter's kidneys slowly began to improve and within six weeks, she completely recovered. I praise God for the peace that passes all understanding. Do you have peace from God today? Have you ever released your tough trials to Him? What did it do for your faith?

by Marilyn

Praises and Prayers

_____

_____

_____

_____

12 ✟ COMFORT

Praise is to the God and Father of our Lord Jesus Christ, the Father of compassion and the God of all comfort, who comforts us in all our troubles, so that we can comfort those in any trouble with the comfort we ourselves have received from God.
2 Corinthian 1:3-4

When my dad passed away, I was grief stricken. I knew that he was a Christian and going to Heaven, but I missed him so much. I missed talking with my dad and hearing his voice. My Christian friends brought food for the family, sent cards and e-mails. I knew they were praying for my family and it helped ease the sorrow. God let me experience the power of their ministry to my aching heart. Now, I know better how to comfort others going through similar situations. Have you ever been comforted in your time of troubles? Sometimes it is a big thing like my dad's death; sometimes it is a small thing like a lost homework paper. Here is the point: we all need the comfort of the Father and comfort from our Christian friends. Whom can you comfort today?

by Marilyn

Praises and Prayers

_____

_____

_____

_____

13 ✝ GOD WILL FIGHT FOR YOU

The LORD will fight for you; you need only to be still.
Exodus 14:14

This verse promises that the LORD will fight for me; I need only to be still. This verse stood out to me when I was reading how God helped Moses, despite the many trials, to lead the Israelites out of Egypt to a safer place. I realized that God has helped my parents accept the fact that I had Cystic Fibrosis (CF). As I grew up, I realized that God would lead me through many trials in my life. God will take care of my needs as long as I follow Him. Letting the Lord fight for me in all of my troubles has really helped me because I don't have to do anything but to stand still. There were times when I fought for myself and I was drained. Sometimes I felt like giving up when I fought the battle against CF by myself. I was exhausted from standing up. When I learned to let go and let the Lord fight for me, I had nothing to worry about. God is constantly looking out for me and fighting to protect me. When I let God lead me and fight for me, I am full of energy and have peace when troubles come my way. God has fought for me in the past and has given me confidence to face anything in the future. Are you letting God fight for you in every area of your life?

by Rebekah

Praises and Prayers

14 ☦ HOPE

***May your unfailing love rest upon us, O LORD,
even as we put our hope in you.***
Psalms 33:22

Have you seen God's intervention in your life? There are many instances where God has intervened and directed my path. For instance, when my daughter was three months old, she was diagnosed with Cystic Fibrosis (CF). Doctors said that Rebekah would probably not live beyond age 13 due to this incurable and progressive disease. God has directly intervened and miraculously restored Rebekah when her lung functions were dangerously low. Rebekah is now a college graduate and a teacher. She was a cheerleader in high school and attended CCA camps. God has a plan for her life and we praise our mighty God for his intervention. All of us at some point will experience what we think is a hopeless situation. We must realize that our hope is in God.   When things seem hopeless where do you turn?

by Marilyn

Praises and Prayers

_____

_____

_____

_____

15 ✞ BLESSINGS

Blessed are those who are persecuted because of righteousness, for theirs is the kingdom of heaven.
Matthew 5:10

The book, *The Heavenly Man*, by Brother Yun and Paul Hattaway, details the dramatic years that Brother Yun spent in a Chinese prison for the crime of preaching and sharing his faith in God. While in prison, Brother Yun received beatings and brutal treatment from the guards. But, God protected Brother Yun and he was miraculously released. Sometimes our trials seem insurmountable, but when we read the testimony of saints that have endured great hardship, it puts our trials in perspective. If they can make it through these difficult things, then I know God will see me through my trials. Are you walking through challenges today because of your faith? God blessed Brother Yun daily. Do you believe that God will bless you?

Praises and Prayers

_____

_____

_____

_____

16 ✟ BE STILL

Be still, and know that I am God.
Psalms 46:10a

Have you ever noticed how noisy it is everywhere? Restaurants sometimes have the music so loud that conversations at the table can't be heard. Most have the radio blaring loud music in the car. At home, the television has the volume on LOUD. It's difficult to focus on God with so much noise. God wants us to spend alone time with Him. In 1 Kings 19:12 God says He speaks in a *gentle whisper.* We must listen closely to hear what He is saying. Being still before God is not the same as doing nothing. At times we need to be still in our quiet time before God, but other times we need to be still in our lives while waiting for God's answer. While being still you do all the things that God has already instructed you to do. Did you ever notice how we intentionally plan to have time with those we care about. It is the same with God. Do you have an intentional quiet time with God? Have you been still before God today in a quiet place so you can receive a message from Him?

Praises and Prayers

_____

_____

_____

_____

17 ✟ GOD'S HELMET AND SWORD

Take the helmet of salvation and the sword of the Spirit, which is the word of God.
Ephesians 6:17

A football helmet can help protect the player from injury, but it can only help if the player actually wears it. Christians have our relationship with God as our helmet, but like the helmet we have to put it on. Just knowing a lot about the helmet, or God, doesn't protect you. You must use it! The world is always trying to penetrate our minds with the ungodly messages. Our faith is what deflects negative messages just as a football helmet protects the player's head. God also gave us a sword – His Word. This is our weapon both for offense and defense. Do you know God's Words in your heart? Just like Jesus, we must fall back on the Word when tempted. Have you put on the helmet of salvation? Are you trusting the Word of God as your sword of protection?

Praises and Prayers

_____

_____

_____

_____

18 ✝ GOD'S WORKS

And we know that in all things God works for the good of those who love him, who have been called according to his purpose.
Romans 8:28

We know that all things in our life are not good. If we focus on God and look to see how God is working in our lives, we can see things from a different perspective.

Note the key words and phrases in this verse:
- All things – what is not covered here? Nothing!
- God works [some translations read "God causes to work"] – Who is working? Almighty God!
- For good – what is good? Jesus said only God is good (Matthew 19), therefore good flows from God.

The verse also has conditions: It is for those (1) who love Him and (2) are called according to His purpose – Christians love Him and each Christian is called.

Are you seeing events in your life as an inconvenience or do you consider that God has a purpose for your trials? What trials are you facing today? Can you see God at work in your life?

Praises and Prayers

_____

_____

_____

_____

19 ✞ TEMPTATION

No temptation has seized you except what is common to man. And God is faithful; he will not let you be tempted beyond what you can bear. But when you are tempted, he will also provide a way out so that you can stand up under it.
1 Corinthians 10:13

When you are in a public room (like a school, theater or a church), there is always an EXIT sign to designate a door for your escape in case of an emergency. God has promised that He will always provide a way of escape when you are tempted. Dr. Craig Etheridge shared in a sermon that God doesn't provide an EXIT just sometimes, but God promises that there will be an EXIT 100% of the time … yes, every single time. For instance, if you are with a group of teens who have decided to do an activity that you know is wrong … you do not have to join. God has given you the power to LEAVE the group and not participate. When tempted by some things, God says the way of escape is just to run – *"flee from sexual immorality"* (1 Corinthians 6:18). What temptations are you facing? Are you ready to look for the EXIT when you are tempted?

Praises and Prayers

_____

_____

_____

_____

20 ✟ POWER

Now to him who is able to do immeasurably more than all we ask or imagine, according to his power that is at work within us.
Ephesians 3:20

At times, life gets overwhelming! Our commitments can keep us so busy that we can't see God at work in our lives – travel to away games, homework assignments, church activities, cheer practice and social events. When you feel overwhelmed, do you want to curl up in a ball and hide? God has given you the power to do the tasks that He has for you. Take a daily TIME OUT so you can have a consistent time with God. You will be amazed! We must realize that there is enough time in each day to do those things to which God has called us. The challenge is to discern what that is. As you spend time with God you will better know His will. Are you listening to Him today?

Praises and Prayers

_____

_____

_____

_____

21 ✞ NEEDS VERSUS WANTS

And my God will meet all your needs according to his glorious riches in Christ Jesus.
Philippians 4:19

It's easy to confuse needs and wants! A want is an item that is not really necessary. For instance, purchasing the newest fashion jeans or the name brand purse isn't a need. A need is something that will sustain your existence - like food, clothes, water and shelter. God has promised to provide all of your needs ... not your wants. Here's a suggestion. Make one list of ten things you really need. Now, make another list with your top ten wants. Evaluate your needs to see if they are really wants. Compare the two lists. Next, ask God to supply your needs, and then truly surrender your wants to Him. Trust Him to supply all you need to make you joyful. Will you praise God today for the needs, and gifts, that He has so richly provided for you?

Praises and Prayers

_____

_____

_____

_____

22 ✝ GOD'S ARMOR

Put on the full armor of God so that you can take your stand against the devil's schemes. For our struggle is not against flesh and blood, but against the rulers, against the authorities, against the powers of this dark world and against the spiritual forces of evil in the heavenly realms.
Ephesians 6:11-12

Harley shared, "This is one of my favorite Bible verses. It talks about the armor of God. It makes me know that God is protecting me."

We are in a great cosmic, spiritual battle between good and evil. Most of the people around us are totally unaware of it. God gives us the discernment to see what is happening. Review the armor God provided. It is listed in Ephesians 6. Don't go into battle without all of your armor. We need to "suit up" each morning by putting on our armor just like a football player puts on pads and a helmet before a game. Cheerleaders don't approach a game or pep rally without being prepared, and Christians shouldn't approach life without the same attention to their preparation. Do you realize that God has prepared you for every life battle that you will encounter?

Praises and Prayers

_____

_____

_____

_____

23 ✝ HOPELESSNESS

But as for me, I will always have hope; I will praise
you more and more.
Psalms 71:14

Have you ever been in a situation that seemed hopeless? I
have. When a doctor told me that I had breast cancer, I
thought my life would end. I felt hopeless. But when I
prayed, I immediately felt the hope that only comes from
God. Hope is related to the confident assurance we have in
God. I knew that even if I died, that my hope was in God. I
prayed at that moment for God's will in my life. And, I
praised God for the peace. Do you have hope (confident
assurance) in God when faced with a hopeless situation?
Or, maybe your situation isn't altogether hopeless, you just
need to make it through the day. The assurance God gives is
the same no matter how big, or how small, the challenge.
Do you have hope from God today?

by Marilyn

Praises and Prayers

_____

_____

_____

_____

24 ✟ ADOPTION

He predestined us to be adopted as his sons through Jesus Christ, in accordance with his pleasure and will.
Ephesians 1:5

My parents went to Korea to pick up eighteen month old Seth. My family had been praying through the tedious adoption process for over a year. My brother actually was an answer to prayer. Even before my little six year-old sister Chloe was born, I had always wanted a little brother, and had prayed for one. I never actually believed that I would have a little brother, I mean; my mom has had three girls already, we all thought for sure she'd have another girl. So through this adoption, it has been God's will for our family, and an answer to prayer to have a baby boy. Throughout this experience, my faith in God has deepened, with the new understanding that God will NEVER break a promise, and that our prayers will be answered in time. Seth was adopted into our family just as we are adopted into the family of God. Seth is ours and we are his. Just as Seth was far off, my parents brought him near, Jesus came to us when we were far off and brought us into the presence of God.   Have you thanked God for adopting you into His family?

by Kaylie

Praises and Prayers

_____

_____

_____

_____

25 ✝ SALVATION

Then I will tell them plainly, "I never knew you. Away from me, you evildoers!"
Matthew 7:23

During the summer of my ninth grade, my team went to a church service each night at the Christian Cheerleaders of America camp. A cheerleader coach gave a dynamic testimony. As a youth she attended all the church functions and knew much about God and the Bible, but a personal relationship with God was lacking. Therefore she was going to spend an eternity in hell. Realizing that she didn't know God, she immediately fell to her knees and asked forgiveness and asked God to come into her heart. That day an inner peace came to her as a result of her new relationship with God. Her testimony described me. I grew up in a Christian home, went to a Christian school and had parents that loved the Lord. Somehow, I had convinced myself that I was going to heaven because I knew the right answers and did Christian things. I finally understood what was missing in my life! I accepted that I needed a personal relationship with my Savior! I almost missed knowing God! He wanted me to hear this testimony! Immediately, I had an inner peace that this world cannot give. Do you have this peace? Do you really know God?

by Rebekah

Praises and Prayers

26 ✟ THE FRUIT OF THE SPIRIT

But the fruit of the Spirit is love, joy, peace, patience, kindness, goodness, faithfulness, gentleness and self-control. Against such things there is no law. Those who belong to Christ Jesus have crucified the sinful nature with its passions and desires. Since we live by the Spirit, let us keep in step with the Spirit. Let us not become conceited, provoking and envying each other.
Galatians 5:22-26

In these verses, we find a list of the characteristics of the fruit of the spirit. Note that the word "fruit" is singular. There is just one. The Spirit of God creates this fruit in us. Galatians tells us what this fruit looks like. It has at least nine traits. These traits can be described as characteristics or actions that come from God alone. So when we look at the trait that we are weakest in, that shows us how mature we are in Christ – we are only as mature as our weakest trait. In the next nine devotions, we will step through each characteristic of the fruit of the Spirit. Are you allowing God to create His fruit in you?

Praises and Prayers

_____

_____

_____

_____

27 ✞ LOVE

But the fruit of the Spirit is love …
from Galatians 5:22

The first characteristic of the fruit of the Spirit is love. Our true model of love is Jesus. He laid down his life for us because he loved us so much! Jesus died on the cross for everyone because we are sinners who couldn't pay the price for our sins! Jesus gave us hope and life when He came down to be a man so that we can become more like Him. We can look to Jesus on earth to see how He loved others. All throughout the New Testament, Jesus reminded and encouraged Christians to love. In John 13:34-35, Jesus said, *A new command I give you: Love one another. As I have loved you, so you must love one another. By this all men will know that you are my disciples, if you love one another.* God wants us to show love to ALL kinds of people, not just to a certain group of people. Love is easy when you get along with other people. Love is harder when you don't get along with others. One good way to show people that you are a Christian is to love everyone regardless of the situation. If you are a Christian, in what ways are you showing love to others? How do you show love to the people who are your friends? How can you show love to strangers?

Praises and Prayers

_____

_____

_____

_____

28 ☩ JOY

But the fruit of the Spirit is … joy …
from Galatians 5:22

Joy is described as having a deep, abiding contentment. This is something that comes from what God has done for us. God saved us from our sin, and wants to have a real relationship with us. God deemed us special enough to love us, and He knows us by name! Of course, we will have troubles that can discourage us and make us angry. Having these emotions is normal, but we must remember that we have an all-powerful God. He can do anything through us and overcome every obstacle we face! I have two diseases, Cystic Fibrosis and diabetes, that frustrate me and can discourage me greatly. When I feel this way, I turn to God to help me have joy. People can tell if you are constantly angry inside or if you have great joy. Proverbs 27:19 states that, *As water reflects a face, so a man's heart reflects the man.* Whatever is inside your heart will eventually show on your face. Are you secretly upset with a family member or friend? Are you jealous of another's achievement? If yes, please seek God and confess (agree with God that this is wrong) this attitude. Ask Him to show you how to rejoice in their achievement. What are some ways you can express joy?

by Rebekah

Praises and Prayers

---

29 ☦ PEACE

But the fruit of the Spirit is … peace … from Galatians 5:22

As Christians, we are called to be at peace. Having peace means that God grants us the ability to remain calm in ALL situations. Our peace must come from God. 1 Corinthians 14:33 reminds us that our God is not a God of disorder but of peace. When our loved ones are arguing with each other or with us, we don't have to get angry and continue to argue with them. When nothing is going our way, we don't have to be in a bad mood. We have the ability that comes from God to have peace in any situation. We can choose to be peaceful so that others can see God in our lives. So, how can you have peace in stressful situations? Claim God's promises. Will you depend on God to bring you peace today?

Praises and Prayers

_____

_____

_____

_____

30 ☩ PATIENCE

But the fruit of the Spirit is ... patience ...
from Galatians 5:22

Patience is another way to be like Christ. I tend to be impatient. I am impatient when another person takes a loooonngg time when we work on a project, or when I have to wait in the doctor's office forever. I get upset that they are not moving on my pace. Recently I have learned to go to God when I get impatient with others. I don't like it when people get impatient with me. God is forever patient with me. He instructs me to be patient with others. James 5:7 says, *Be patient, then, brothers, until the Lord's coming. See how the farmer waits for the land to yield its valuable crop and how patient he is for the autumn and spring rains.* When you have patience, you are not rushing things that could cause you to make mistakes along the way. When I rushed my homework projects in school, I made many mistakes. I had to spend more time to undo my mistakes. When I practiced patience and took my time, I only had to do the project once. There is much satisfaction in doing things slower and the right way. What things cause you to be impatient? Do others get impatient with you? Have you asked God to help you with your impatience?

by Rebekah

Praises and Prayers

_____

_____

_____

_____

31 ✝ KINDNESS

But the fruit of the Spirit is ... kindness ...
from Galatians 5:22

Some of the synonyms for kindness are respectful, grace, favor, mercy, and service. A little kindness can go a long way. Kindness can brighten someone's day. John 4:1-26 tells the story of Jesus being kind to the Samaritan woman. Because Jesus was kind to this woman, He was able to witness to her, and the woman became a follower of Christ. Without Jesus being kind, this woman may not have believed in God. In a fast pace society, do we take the time to show kindness to all sorts of people? Do we give grace to those who cut us off or shove us to the side with their actions? How often do we serve others on a daily basis? How can your kind actions change someone's day or life?

Praises and Prayers

_____

_____

_____

_____

32 ✝ GOODNESS

But the fruit of the Spirit is ... goodness ...
from Galatians 5:22

Goodness is another characteristic of the fruit of the Spirit. Some synonyms of goodness are decency, honesty, and rightness. Being good can be a hard thing, but we need to be good so that people can see a difference in our lives as we walk with God. If we don't portray the characteristics of Christ, we are not letting God shine in our lives, and we are not being a positive witness for Christ. We must pray for God to show His goodness through us. We are called to be good wherever we are – at school, at home, or out with friends. Also, we can ask ourselves some questions to see if our actions or choices reflect the goodness of Christ. Is what I say or wear appropriate? Anyone can be honest without hurting another person's feelings. How often do I tell the truth to others? Are my actions honorable before God?

Praises and Prayers

_____

_____

_____

_____

33 ✞ FAITHFULNESS

But the fruit of the Spirit is ...faithfulness ...
from Galatians 5:22

Faith is one of the main traits we should have as Christians! Without faith, we can't believe in Christ. With faith in Christ, anything is possible! As Jesus said in Matthew 17:20b, *I tell you the truth, if you have faith as small as mustard seed, you can say to this mountain, 'Move from here to there' and it will move. Nothing will be impossible for you.* Also, God wants us to have a childlike faith as written in Matthew 19:13-14. These verses state, *Then little children were brought to Jesus for him to place his hands on them and pray for them. But the disciples rebuked those who brought them. Jesus said, "Let the little children come to me, and do not hinder them, for the kingdom of heaven belongs to such as these."* I am a preschool teacher in a Christian environment. Whenever I teach about God, the children are so excited, and they are awed by Jesus' miracles. I think God wants us to continue being excited and awed by what He did for us, what He is doing for us, and what He will do for us in the future! Have you lost your excitement for God? What can you do to keep being excited about God? Can you focus on God's faithfulness?

by Rebekah

Praises and Prayers

_____

_____

_____

_____

34 ✝ GENTLENESS

But the fruit of the Spirit is … gentleness …
from Galatians 5:22-23

Gentleness can be described as being considerate. This is so hard for me to do sometimes. I have to admit I tend to think about my needs before others. I confess that sometimes I am just not considerate toward others. I expect the other person to meet my need instead of me meeting the other person's need. This is wrong and leads to much discord! If every Christian meets another's need, then everyone's need will be met. This is the way the early church served each other as shown in Acts.

The definition for gentleness includes not being harsh. This caused me to think about the many times I have been harsh in my own life. Sometimes I was harsh on material things like slamming doors out of anger – but it wasn't the thing that made me angry, it was another person. Sometimes what I said was harsh and hurt another person's feelings. I never felt good about it later. Do you have temper tantrums? What are the ways you can be gentle with both your things and other people?

by Rebekah

Praises and Prayers

_____

_____

_____

_____

35 ✟ SELF-CONTROL

But the fruit of the Spirit is … self-control …
from Galatians 5:22-23

Self-control is the last characteristic of the fruit of the Spirit mentioned in Scripture. This has always been the hardest for me. Growing up, sometimes I had trouble focusing on my homework. Sometimes I waited until the last minute to do a school project and didn't do a good job because I hurried through it. Over time, I learned to write down what I need to do first and work my way down the list. I also find it hard to control my emotions or anger in an argument and I end up saying things I regret. Sometimes I just need to stop a disagreement to cool down. When I take the time to control my anger, I can be more sensible and find a solution that works for all people involved. In the Bible, there are many verses that encourage us to have self-control. James 1:20 says to control our anger *for man's anger does not bring about the righteous life that God desires*, and James 3:1-12 says to watch what you say. What are the areas of self-control where you need to focus?

by Rebekah

Praises and Prayers

_____

_____

_____

_____

36 ✟ PRAYER

"Again, I tell you that if two of you on earth agree about anything you ask for, it will be done for you by my Father in heaven. For where two or three come together in my name, there am I with them."
Matthew 18:19-20

Some time ago, I thought I was only going for a regular checkup for Cystic Fibrosis. I regularly do pulmonary function tests (PFTs). These tests measure the lung's capacity to take in and exhale air. My lung functions were in the thirty percentile range which is dangerously low. One of the doctors introduced the possibility of having a double lung transplant in the future if my lung functions continued at less than thirty percent. My PFTs have remained in the thirty percent range for ten years. The power of united prayer from our friends and family has worked. Our prayer chain extends from coast to coast and even halfway around the world to friends in India. The CF doctor is amazed with my activity level despite my low lung functions. I hold a part time job, exercise daily, and stay active in my church. Normally, a person with low lung functions is in declining health and needs oxygen and many hospital stays. United prayers work! Do you believe in the power of prayer?

by Rebekah

Praises and Prayers

_____

_____

_____

_____

37 ✝ TALKING TO GOD

Be joyful in hope, patient in affliction, faithful in prayer.
Romans 12:12

The word "hope" in the New Testament means "confident assurance." Substitute that phrase for "hope" each time you see it in the Bible. We are to be joyful, or rejoice, because we have a confident assurance. Look at the context of this verse in Romans 12. Paul is telling us how to live – how to *offer your bodies as living sacrifices, holy and pleasing to God - this is your spiritual act of worship.* Then he says to be *patient in affliction.* "Patient" means to persevere or "hang tight," or to endure or carry bravely and calmly. "Affliction" can mean tribulation or stress – it carries the idea of being "pressed." So when our situation presses us, we are to endure bravely and calmly. How? Because we know in our hearts that Jesus led the way. Finally, the verse tells us to be *faithful in prayer.* The Greek word can also mean "devoted" and carries the idea of "adhering." Prayer is just talking to God, so this part of the verse could be interpreted as saying, "Glue yourself to your conversations with God!" Do you rejoice because you are confident in Christ? Do you "bear up" under pressure? Do you pray only when you are facing a difficult situation? Praying is talking to God. Have you been faithful in prayer today?

Praises and Prayers

---

38 ✝ DEALING WITH TOUGH TIMES

Be joyful always; pray continually; give thanks in all circumstances, for this is God's will for you in Christ Jesus.
1 Thessalonians 5:16-18

Can you really be joyful always? What if I am not happy about what is happening to me? "Happy" is an emotion. It comes and goes with how we feel or with what we have experienced. "Joy" is a mindset. It is a choice. It is not determined by how we feel or by our situation. Jesus *endured the cross for the joy that was set before Him* (Hebrews 12:2b). Was Jesus happy about what happened on the cross? Do we let the circumstance of life determine our happiness? Can we be joyful in a difficult situation? The key is to be continuously in the presence of God, talking to Him about our experiences, and giving thanks no matter what. Others are watching us as we witness to them and share our faith in God. Have you given thanks for the situation that you are in today? Can you be joyful in a difficult situation knowing that God is in control?

Praises and Prayers

_____

_____

_____

_____

39 ✟ GUARD YOUR HEART

Above all else, guard your heart, for it is the wellspring of life.
Proverbs 4:23

The Bible tells us in several places to guard our hearts, and to be careful of the things that we read, see or hear. What goes in your mind will eventually come out through your words and actions! *The good man brings good things out of the good stored up in him, and the evil man brings evil things out of the evil stored up in him* (Matthew 12:35). So, think about how you spend your spare time. On your way home from school, what type of music do you listen to. Much of today's secular music has angry words. Could you choose instead to listen to Christian music with uplifting words? Think about the books that you are reading. Are the books worthy of your time? When you go to a theater, do you carefully select the movies that you watch? The Bible challenges us to guard our hearts? So, how can you guard your heart? Do you evaluate books, movies or music at their core level? Try to formulate in one sentence what the message of each song, book or movie is. Is it something you would be proud to share with Jesus? What are you doing to guard your heart today?

Praises and Prayers

_____

_____

_____

_____

40 ✝ MEMORIZE SCRIPTURE

I have hidden your word in my heart that I might not sin against you.
Psalms 119:11

When we hide something, we have put it somewhere for safe keeping and we know where to find it. The Bible verses that we memorize are tucked away in our hearts. We hide them away in our minds like a treasure. When we meditate on Scripture, it is like taking our treasure out of hiding and admiring it. We can understand God's commands better when we have memorized them. How can we identify a sin against God if we don't read and memorize the Scriptures? When we fill up our minds with Scripture, we can easily carry it with us and access it whenever we need it. This verse promises that when we know Scripture it will work to prevent sin in our life. I have found that God brings the perfect Scripture to my mind at just the right time. Have you hidden Scripture in your heart? Do you have a plan for regularly memorizing Scripture? Who holds you accountable for memorizing Scripture? Could you and a friend memorize Scripture together? How about memorizing one Scripture per week with your Cheer Team?

Praises and Prayers

_____

_____

_____

_____

41 ✞ MEDITATION

Let me understand the teaching of your precepts;
then I will meditate on your wonders.
Psalms 119:27

Meditation is when we reflect deeply on a subject. It helps to be in a quiet place. A good place to meditate on Scripture would be in your room or outside on the patio. Meditation requires us to think over Scripture while seeking what insights God's Spirit may provide. There are many ways to approach meditation, so let's look at just one. Memorize a Scripture verse, or verses. Go over it in your mind one word at a time thinking about what each word means. If there are pronouns, substitute I, me, mine, etc., for the more general pronouns. You can even put your own name in place of those pronouns. The goal is to see yourself in the Bible verse. Visualize what the verse is describing. Are there sounds? Are there smells? Was it warm or cold? Try to put yourself in that place so you can experience the reality of the verse. When we meditate on Scripture, we focus on the great and mighty God who intervenes in our lives daily. Have you made time to meditate on the wonders of God?

Praises and Prayers

_____

_____

_____

_____

My Prayer Closet

There has been a change in me!
I feel as though I've been set free!

For a time, God wasn't number one in my life,
I had succumbed to sin and strife.

Prayer was not on my lips very often ,
My cold, hard heart needed to soften.

This went on for a few years,
There were empty feelings and many fears.

Then I remembered my prayer closet again.
This was my chance to let God reign.

To ask Him into my heart once more,
For me to open up the door.

This is where it's just God and me,
A place where broken and humbled I plea,

For mercy, forgiveness, grace, and love,
Although deserving none from above.

I can sing, praise Him, and worship, too.
Thank Him and confess sins He already knew.

I ask Him to watch over me,
And especially watch over my family.

Please save the lost people everywhere,
This is my most urgent prayer.

God never went away, you see,
The only one who moved was me.

Yet through it all,
God is faithful when we call.

He will never leave nor forsake,
So God sent His Son, our sins to take.

So if you're feeling lonely and blue,
You better meet God in the closet too!

© Beth Perry . Used by permission.

42 ✞ UNITE IN PRAYER

Therefore confess your sins to each other and pray for each other so that you may be healed. The prayer of a righteous man is powerful and effective.

James 5:16

I have been part of a Sunday School class where we pray specifically for needs of those who are present that day. It is so comforting to hear a room full of people lift up your prayer needs to God. Not only that, but God promises us power when we agree together in prayer. We have experienced answers to prayers that are beyond all expectations. Are you part of a group that prays regularly? When sharing prayer requests in groups we need to follow a few guidelines. Share the essence of the request, not all of the details. Respect privacy – do not let prayer requests become the subject of gossip. Don't monopolize the group – let everyone have an opportunity. Sincerely seek the will of God on these matters. Do you make time with your cheer group to pray each time you are together?

by Marilyn

Praises and Prayers

_____

_____

_____

_____

43 ✟ UNEXPECTED ANSWERS

Jesus replied, "You do not realize now what I am doing, but later you will understand."
John 13:7

Have you every prayed for something and the answer from God was not what you wanted or expected? About two years ago, my dad's friend who also is a firefighter had a baby boy named Cooper. Cooper was born very sick and we prayed every day for the doctors to find out what was wrong with him. I praised God for knowing what was best for the baby and asked that God would heal him. Cooper died at nine weeks old. Baby Cooper made such an impact on so many people in his short life and still does. Money is being raised for other sick babies because of his story. Cooper may have not been healed on earth but he lives in Heaven now. Sometimes prayers aren't answered exactly as we would like, but God's plan is greater. I learned that from Cooper's life. Will you praise God today for answers to prayers even when you don't understand?

by Harley

Praises and Prayers

44 ✟ CHOICES – LIVING DIFFERENTLY

So I tell you this, and insist on it in the Lord, that you must no longer live as the Gentiles do, in the futility of their thinking ... You were taught, with regard to your former way of life, to put off your old self, which is being corrupted by its deceitful desires; to be made new in the attitude of your minds; and to put on the new self, created to be like God in true righteousness and holiness.
Ephesians 4:17, 22-24

The moment we surrender our hearts to Christ is the moment we are changed FOREVER! We are no longer trapped into harmful and deadly lives. We are set free through Christ's love! We have an inner peace and love and goodness in our hearts. The Holy Spirit will help us live like Christ. As Christians, we have knowledge of how to live a better life. As we study and know more about God, we become more mature in His ways. We shouldn't act like non-believers, but as people passionately living for God! The more we know God, the more we are aware of our sins and old ways of thinking. We know how to love better and to sin less. Is there an area in your life that is not dedicated to God?

Praises and Prayers

_____

_____

_____

_____

45 ✟ ATTITUDE

You were taught, with regard to your former way of life, to put off your old self, which is being corrupted by its deceitful desires; to be made new in the attitude of your minds; and to put on the new self, created to be like God in true righteousness and holiness.
Ephesians 4:22-24

I can be a witness and share about God to all the people around me especially when I am in the hospital. It is very easy when things just aren't going my way to be angry and feel sorry for myself. I have learned that negativity spreads fast and doesn't make anyone feel good. Having a positive attitude makes everyone feel better and leads to a healthier life. This verse reminded me that I can always have hope because God has given me a "new self." The hospital staff is actually sad each time when I am finally released from my many hospitalizations. The nurses enjoy being around me because of my God-given joy. When people ask me why I have so much joy, I just tell them that God is my source of happiness. Your attitude does make a difference! Do you spread negativity to others by your bad moods? Are people happy or sad when you leave?

by Rebekah

Praises and Prayers

_____

_____

_____

_____

46 ✞ CAREFUL WORDS

Do not let any unwholesome talk come out of your mouths, but only what is helpful for building others up according to their needs, that it may benefit those who listen.
Be kind and compassionate to one another, forgiving each other, just as in Christ God forgave you.
Ephesians 4:29,32

You have heard the saying, "Sticks and stones may break my bones, but words will never hurt me." This just isn't true – it is wishful thinking. Words can be VERY hurtful!!! Mean words are very hard to forget. You can NEVER take back the hurtful things you say. Kind words can make your spirit soar and encourages others. Calming words can help stop someone from being stressed or angry. I encourage you to consider what you say to anyone that crosses your path and especially the words that you say to your friends. Do your words hurt people's feelings or encourage them? Is the tone of your voice bitter and angry? Are you tearing down someone to others? How kind are you to others? Do you quickly forgive? Are you careful with words?

Praises and Prayers

----

47 ✝ IMITATORS OF GOD

Be imitators of God, therefore, as dearly loved children and live a life of love, just as Christ loved us and gave himself up for us as a fragrant offering and sacrifice to God.
Ephesians 5:1-2

Our actions and thoughts should reflect the same attitude Jesus had when He was on earth. We are called to glorify God in everything we do in our lives. Christians are called to love others like Jesus does. This verse reminds me of a trend when I was growing up. There was this bracelet that had the initials of WWJD which reminded Christians to ask ourselves this question before we did anything: "What Would Jesus Do?" I loved wearing this bracelet because it helped me to stop and think. For example, if someone made me angry, the bracelet helped remind me not to respond in anger but to address the issue out of love. If I was tempted to gossip, the bracelet reminded me that I needed to keep myself from spreading rumors about others. This WWJD bracelet helped me to strive to be an imitator of Christ at ALL times. What are some ways to remind yourself to be an imitator of Christ in all your situations?

by Rebekah

Praises and Prayers

_____

_____

_____

_____

48 ✝ IMPURITY

But among you there must not be even a hint of sexual immorality, or of any kind of impurity, or of greed, because these are improper for God's holy people. Nor should there be obscenity, foolish talk or coarse joking, which are out of place, but rather thanksgiving.

Ephesians 5:3-4

Christians need to live a pure life to glorify God. One way to glorify God is to honor Him with our bodies. When people are dating, showing affection is a natural thing to do. God wants us to be pure and not have any sort of sexual immorality in us. *Every Woman's Battle: Discovering God's Plan for Sexual and Emotional Fulfillment* (*The Every Man Series*) by Shannon Etheridge and Stephen Arterburn discusses how to be pure. They give tips such as wearing a promise ring, being in group dates, and keeping the alone time with a boyfriend to a minimum so you won't be tempted. Have you considered doing a Bible study with your boyfriend? Christians must speak and act in ways that point people to God. How do you act or talk when you are with your friends?

Praises and Prayers

_____

_____

_____

_____

49 ✞ DO NOT BE DECEIVED

Let no one deceive you with empty words, for because of such things God's wrath comes on those who are disobedient. Therefore do not be partners with them. For you were once darkness, but now you are light in the Lord. Live as children of light.
Ephesians 5:6-8

We see so many advertisements that promise us something but can't fulfill that promise. There are so many unfulfilled promises from billboards, books, magazines, newspapers, news stations, radio and the internet. We are promised that if we use this shampoo, our hair will look beautiful and we will get more dates; if you drink this soda, you are fun; if you use a certain toothpaste, your teeth will be sparkling white and everyone will notice you. I have tried using the shampoo, soda, and toothpaste, but I didn't get what the commercials promised. I am tempted to listen to what the world promises through the false ads, but I can't let myself be deceived. The only way to avoid deception is by studying and reading what the Bible says. Praying helps me not to be deceived. God always reveals the truth to me. Where do you find truth?

by Rebekah

Praises and Prayers

50 ✞ BE WISE

Be very careful, then, how you live - not as unwise but as wise, making the most of every opportunity, because the days are evil. Therefore do not be foolish, but understand what the Lord's will is.
Ephesians 5:15-17

Let's face it. Every day we hear about all the evil in the news. As time goes on, the world will have more evil. When I was growing up, I remember my teachers, my parents, and my parent's friends saying that they could not believe how evil the world is getting or that things were not this bad when they were growing up. I groaned every time they said this, but now I am an adult, and I am saying the exact same thing that they did. Things HAVE gotten worse in my lifetime. You probably will be saying the same thing when you are an adult. In Revelation, there are prophecies that say times will continue to worsen until the second coming of Christ. The only way Christians can be wise is to study the Bible. I love reading the book of Proverbs because this book helps to define a wise man and a foolish man. The wise will witness (tell what they have seen and experienced) to others. The days are evil and we need to reach everybody that we can. Are you making the most of every opportunity?

by Rebekah

Praises and Prayers

_____

_____

_____

_____

51 ✞ THANKFULNESS

Always giving thanks to God the Father for everything, in the name of our Lord Jesus Christ.
Ephesians 5:20

One November years ago, each day leading to Thanksgiving I started to list one thing for which I was thankful. Next, I gave the praise to God for the blessings for which I was thankful on that particular day. Some days, I could list many things I was thankful for, but others days I struggled to find only a few things to express thankfulness. On Thanksgiving Day, I looked at all the things I had listed and I gave thanks to God for what He had given me. I realized how blessed I was, and that most people didn't have these things I was thankful for – such as a loving family that lives nearby, good health, the freedom to worship God, and tons of material things. This exercise made me think about how often I take things for granted. Now, I do my best to be thankful for something each day - even in a bad situation. A bad situation can teach me something if I look for the lesson. I encourage you to write down what you are thankful for every day for a week. You may be surprised at how much you are blessed by God. Why not start your thankfulness list today?

by Rebekah

Praises and Prayers

_____

_____

_____

_____

52 ✟ ACTIONS PORTRAY YOUR FAITH

What good is it, my brothers, if a man claims to have faith but has no deeds? Can such faith save him? Suppose a brother or sister is without clothes and daily food. If one of you says to him, "Go, I wish you well; keep warm and well fed," but does nothing about his physical needs, what good is it? In the same way, faith by itself, if it is not accompanied by action, is dead.
James 2:14-17

Have you noticed some friends say one thing, but do something else instead? For example, have you ever seen someone say that they will not gossip but you turn around and hear them share negative comments about a friend? This is how some Christians act. People say that they are Christians but they never do godly things. Pay attention to 1 Timothy 4:16 which says to *Watch your life and doctrine closely. Persevere in them, because if you do, you will save both yourself and your hearers*. This encourages Christians to reflect God at ALL times in our public and private actions. Do your actions reflect your knowledge of God? When you are around people, does what you say and do reflect God? When you are alone in your room, do your thoughts and actions reflect God? Does your walk match your talk?

Praises and Prayers

---

53 ✞ THE BIBLE MATTERS

*Direct me in the path of your commands, for there
I find delight.*
Psalms 119:35

Psalms 119 is the longest chapter in the Bible. It teaches us why the Bible matters. Dr. Scott Maze says, "The Bible has sin-killing power, but it also has mind-blowing beauty!" Hebrews calls the Word of God a two-edged sword that can test our motives and emotions. Not only that, the Word challenges areas of our lives that are not pleasing to God. *"Is not my word like fire,"* declares the LORD, *"and like a hammer that breaks a rock in pieces?"* (Jeremiah 23:29) The Word describes itself as a fire that burns inside believers! This fiery truth wants to get out and warm those around us. His holy hammer breaks down our motives and reveals our hearts' intent. For these statements to be true in our lives, we must experience the Bible, not just simply read it. Jesus said He sent the Holy Spirit to live in us that we might know Him in a real and personal way. When we are still before God in prayer and meditation, the Spirit confirms His Word in us and it becomes real to us. Do you make time to delight in the Word of God? Do you let God build His character in you through daily intake of His Word?

Praises and Prayers

_____

_____

_____

_____

54 ✝ WITHOUT COMPLAINING

Do everything without complaining or arguing.
Philippians 2:14

In 2011, one of my frequent hospital stays was the most challenging time I had ever experienced. My kidneys began quickly shutting down due to a reaction to a medication. All I wanted to do was sit still so that I wouldn't feel sick to my stomach when I moved. I was put on a special diet to help my kidneys. Due to the nausea and a limited bland diet, I barely ate and lost weight. My kidneys were almost to the point of requiring dialysis. Apparently, there was little to be done but to wait and see if they would heal themselves. I was so discouraged. I decided to obey God and *do everything without complaining or arguing*. Romans 12:12 says to be joyful always and thankful. God is always active in those who are faithful. James 1:2-4 reminded me that trials can sharpen anyone's faith. I wanted to live out these verses because they helped me to tell others about God. I determined to be more positive and joyful to the people around me during these difficult trials Some nurses told me that my joyful attitude helped them have a better day. Also, nurses take me serious when I do complain. I encourage you to choose a positive attitude at all times. Having a joyful heart helps you to overcome anything! The source of my joy is God! He can be yours too! How can you be thankful, or positive, in your trials?

by Rebekah

Praises and Prayers

_____

_____

_____

_____

55 ✞ CHOICES

Don't you know that you yourselves are God's temple and that God's Spirit lives in you?
1 Corinthians 3:16

There are some Bible verses that have encouraged me to take better care of myself despite having Cystic Fibrosis, diabetes and allergies. I am God's temple and God's Spirit lives in me. I am not my own; I was bought at a price. Therefore, I should honor God with my body. As a Christian, the Holy Spirit lives in me. I need to take care of my body. I need to do everything I can to take care of myself so I can be healthy. I must have plenty of rest, do all my treatments and take all of my medications. If I don't take care of myself, I will be doing damage to my lungs. This would not honor God and, therefore, hurt my Christian testimony because I wouldn't have the energy to tell others about Christ. What are the ways you are not taking care of your body? The answers can be anything! Are you getting enough sleep? Are you eating healthy foods? Too little exercise can be as dangerous as too much exercise. What are the ways you are taking care of your body?

by Rebekah

Praises and Prayers

_____

_____

_____

_____

56 ✟ ROCK SOLID FOUNDATION

Therefore everyone who hears these words of mine and puts them into practice is like a wise man who built his house on the rock. The rain came down, the streams rose, and the winds blew and beat against that house; yet it did not fall, because it had its foundation on the rock.
Matthew 7:24-25

Cheerleaders know the importance of a strong base. The person at the base often will hold another girl at arm's length over her head supporting her in a Liberty or Scorpion position. Always, the physically strongest cheerleader is on the bottom of the mount as the base. The theory is simple: the girl on the top wants a strong foundation. When weak members are on the bottom, the girls will tumble and fall. Do you have a strong foundation? Christians understand this concept very well. The Rock of our Salvation, Jesus Christ, is all the foundation that is needed. Without a strong base, it is difficult to stand firm as a Christian and avoid the tumbles and falls of life. Are your feet planted firmly on the rock solid foundation of Jesus Christ?

Praises and Prayers

_____

_____

_____

_____

57 ✟ CHOOSING YOUR FRIENDS

Do not be misled: "Bad company corrupts good character."
1 Corinthians 15:33

If we want to know who we truly are as a person, look to see who our friends are. You get along with the people who are most similar to you. Do your friends always talk back to adults and always seem to be in trouble? Do your friends gossip and lie? Do your friends love and support each other and their family? What do your friends believe in? Do they go to church? If you hang out with people who make bad choices, you will start thinking those choices are okay, and start making those choices as well. The opposite also works – friends that make good choices encourage you to make good choices. At a student assembly, the minister asked a person to stand in a chair, then he asked two other students to stand on each side of her. He then asked if it would be easier for the student on the chair to pull the other two up, or easier for the two on the floor to pull the one on the chair down. If the one on the chair is a good influence and tries to lift everyone around her it is frequently doomed to failure. It also shows how strong bad influences (represented by the two standing on the floor) can be when they surround us. Christians must stand together to hold one another up. Who are the ones surrounding you?

Praises and Prayers

_____

_____

_____

_____

58 ✝ DO YOUR ACTIONS MAKE OTHERS STUMBLE?

But if anyone causes one of these little ones who believe in me to sin, it would be better for him to have a large millstone hung around his neck and to be drowned in the depths of the sea.
Matthew 18:6

We never know who we are influencing. We may be influencing someone we have never met. For example, if you are a cheerleader, your influence can reach the WHOLE school because you are performing cheers at games and pep rallies. But we aren't watched only on these occasions, people are always watching us to see if we are "for real." If we treat others badly, our actions may affect those who see us in a negative way. If we treat others with kindness and respect, we may touch someone's life in a way that we can never know. Our good actions can encourage others to be good and strive for greatness. We may not know how we influenced someone until years later. How can we look for ways to encourage others? Encouraging others can be as small as saying, "Hi," or talking with them, or even opening the door for someone. Could you pray with your friend? The choice is ours, or, more personally, yours. You can be a good influence or bad influence. What will you choose?

Praises and Prayers

_____
_____
_____
_____

59 ✟ PEER PRESSURE

I can do everything through him who gives me strength.
Philippians 4:13

This verse in Philippians has always been my favorite Bible verse. When I am facing difficult issues in high school, God brings this verse to my mind and heart. The main challenge that I face is peer pressure. I struggle with being like Jesus often, especially when I am more concerned about the "needs" and wants of this world. I have difficulty loving others above myself. Many times I am only concerned for my needs and wants. When I feel like I cannot do anything on my own, I go back and read this verse. God gives me the strength every single time to overcome the challenges that I am facing. Are you struggling with peer pressure? Do you think that you have to follow the group? Do you really think that the peer group is more important than God? God promises that He will give you the strength to do everything that He has commanded you to do. Can you rely on God's strength when you are faced with a challenge today?

by Kaylie

Praises and Prayers

_____

_____

_____

_____

60 ✞ CHARACTER

She is clothed with strength and dignity; she can laugh at the days to come. She speaks with wisdom, and faithful instruction is on her tongue. She watches over the affairs of her household and does not eat the bread of idleness. Her children arise and call her blessed; her husband also, and he praises her: "Many women do noble things, but you surpass them all."
Proverbs 31:25-29

A good leader has good characteristics. A good leader respects herself and is happy. She gets her wisdom from God and is very knowledgeable whenever she speaks. A good leader is faithful to God. She works hard. The people she leads think very highly of her. Proverbs 29:2 states: W*hen the righteous thrive, the people rejoice; when the wicked rule, the people groan*, and Proverbs 29:4 says: *By justice a king gives a country stability, but one who is greedy for bribes tears it down.* These verses remind me that a good leader brings joy and stability and a bad leader brings misery and tears down everything. What does a bad leader do in a school setting? What effect does a bad leader bring to the school? Have you seen what a good leader does and the effects of a good leader? What kind of leader are you?

Praises and Prayers

_____

_____

_____

_____

61 ✞ LEADERSHIP

Charm is deceptive, and beauty is fleeting; but a woman who fears the LORD is to be praised.
Proverbs 31:30

Many people think a leader should be pretty and charming enough to be popular. However, a true leader chases after God's heart and encourages others to do this same thing. One of the definitions of fear is to have a reverential awe. Reverence means to have honor or respect. Awe means to wonder. This verse says that a woman who honors and respects God and wonders at His glory is to be praised. Beauty doesn't last forever. We eventually will get older and look older, too. We shouldn't strive to look like models or celebrities to receive praise. Christians should be praised for our love for our great and mighty God. What do you spend your time doing? Do you spend more time worrying about looking pretty and wearing the most fashionable clothes? Or, do you spend your time reading God's Word, talking to Him, and doing things that bring God glory? What have you done today to bring glory to God?

Praises and Prayers

_____

_____

_____

_____

62 ✝ WORK HARD

She selects wool and flax and works with eager hands. She is like the merchant ships, bringing her food from afar. She gets up while it is still dark; she provides food for her family and portions for her servant girls. She considers a field and buys it; out of her earnings she plants a vineyard. She sets about her work vigorously; her arms are strong for her tasks.

Proverbs 31:13-17

A good leader is a hard worker and plans ahead. She sets goals and gets things done. A leader understands that work can last all day but she knows that work can pay off for her team. Work can bring character. I have found that when I work hard at doing things, like taking time to do my homework, I will learn something and get a better grade. Colleges do look at grades from high school. High school grades are what determine college acceptance. Good grades require hard work! After working hard on a project, I feel like I have accomplished something great. In what areas do you need to work harder? Are you setting goals so the work will be accomplished?

by Rebekah

Praises and Prayers

_____

_____

_____

_____

63 ☩ ROLE MODEL

Train a child in the way he should go, and when he is old he will not turn from it.
Proverbs 22:6

Kaylie's parents, James and Valerie, provide a Christian example by pointing their children to Christ. They read the Bible, attend church and pray together as a family. Kaylie writes, "My parents are my role models because they have had the greatest impact on my life. They have taught me and shown me that God's way is the right path for my life. My parents have always been there for me, and especially when I needed someone to stand up for me. They make me strive to be more like Christ every day." Are you striving to be more like Christ? Do you have a role model in your life who helps you train? It's your responsibility to apply the training to your life. People are investing in our lives daily so we will have a strong foundation for the future. Have you thought about thanking that person (or persons) for their training?

Praises and Prayers

_____

_____

_____

_____

64 ✟ GOOD WORKS

For we are God's workmanship, created in Christ Jesus to do good works, which God prepared in advance for us to do.
Ephesians 2:10

We often wonder what God has planned for us in the future. Much energy is focused on which college to attend and which profession to choose. Perhaps focusing on God's plan for today is just as important as focusing on plans for the future. Scripture says that God has prepared in advance works for us do to. God has equipped us with everything we need to accomplish His work. The Biblical principle is: The person who is faithful in small things will be rewarded with greater responsibility (see Luke 19:17). Are we faithful in the small things God calls us to do? We must see the small things as training for bigger things. Small things include kindness to others, faithfulness in assignments, and consistent prayer life. List some other small things. What are you doing today that will minister to others and point them to God? Is there anything in your life that is preventing you from doing God's work?

Praises and Prayers

_____

_____

_____

_____

65 ✝ GOD HAS PLANS FOR ME

"For I know the plans I have for you," declares the LORD, "plans to prosper you and not to harm you, plans to give you hope and a future."
Jeremiah 29:11

During difficult times, we often think that God is punishing us or that we are simply forgotten. But, that's just not true! God promises that His plans are to prosper you and give you hope. Does that mean that everyone will be wealthy and live a life without sickness or trials? Of course not! It means that God has plans for you beyond anything that can be imagined. God's plans are to give you hope and a future. Here's a question: If you trusted God with your eternal destination of Heaven, can you trust Him to guide you through the trials of today? Jesus said He is the same yesterday, today and forever (see Hebrews 13:8) – you can depend on Him in the future because you can see His actions in the past. Do you trust God with your future?

Praises and Prayers

_____

_____

_____

_____

What Will I Do?

How exciting, a trip to Lubbock in my first car!
It's only 100 miles − not very far.

Only God knew the event to take place
Soon angels would be dispatched to act out God's grace.

Right in front of us a car has rolled in our lane,
They weren't watching – the only way to explain.

We moved to the next lane to miss the car,
They moved in our lane, this is bizarre!

I brace for the crash, he turns the car for a broadside impact.
There's only a split second, no time to react.

I must have passed out before the collision,
We were thrown out on the road, not something I would envision.

Don't move her, her neck could be broken.
Am I dreaming, or did I hear these words spoken.

The lady placed her satin-lined coat over my face,
It's as if I'm in another time and another place.

Is this it, God, will I be with you today?
This would be a good time to pray.

My relationship with God wasn't there yet,
But His angels had been dispatched, don't forget.

In and out of consciousness; the noisy siren blares
The ambulance races to the hospital – I'm convinced there were prayers.

All of a sudden, the smelling salts take effect,
I'm free to go, I've been checked.

When I look back on that day long ago,
I realize God's love and grace were at full flow.

"God saved you for a purpose," my grandmother said,
"You could have just as easily been dead."

Yes, in the blink of an eye, I could have died,
But God's protection was provided.

Why me, oh God, why have you spared me?
What is my purpose - this I plea.

What is your purpose? Has God shown you?
Have you asked Him, "What will I do?"

© Beth Perry . Used by permission.

66 ✟ BE READY TO SHARE

But in your hearts set apart Christ as Lord. Always be prepared to give an answer to everyone who asks you to give the reason for the hope that you have. But do this with gentleness and respect, keeping a clear conscience, so that those who speak maliciously against your good behavior in Christ may be ashamed of their slander.
1 Peter 3:15-16

This verse says to ALWAYS be ready to share your faith! People will see you as someone different if you are a Christian who is constantly faithful to God. Your actions show what you believe. On many occasions, people in my life ask me why I am so happy. Even at the grocery store I frequent, the cashier has told me that my face always has a smile. Depending on the situation, I talk about God and how He always makes me happy and has blessed my life. Many times, a nurse will notice my cheerful heart when I am in the hospital because I am very sick with Cystic Fibrosis. This gives me an opportunity to share. We need to be ready at ALL times to give our testimony in one minute or be able to have a long detailed discussion. Have you thought through your testimony? Have you written it down? Can you give a quick version in one minute?

by Rebekah

Praises and Prayers

_____

_____

_____

_____

67 ✝ ACTIONS PORTRAY YOUR FAITH

But someone will say, "You have faith; I have deeds." Show me your faith without deeds, and I will show you my faith by what I do ... As the body without the spirit is dead, so faith without deeds is dead.

James 2:18, 26

There are so many people that say that they are Christians but their actions show that they are not. These so-called Christians act like non-believers even though they claim to be a Christian. Because of this sad fact, many non-believers won't ever attend church or give their life to Christ. The Bible even says that demons believe in God and shudder! As Christians, our faith should dictate our actions. We cannot have one without the other. If we say we love others, we should act like we love others instead of tearing them down. Do your actions portray what you believe? What have you done today to show a friend at school or a family member that you are a Christian?

Praises and Prayers

_____

_____

_____

_____

68 ✞ SERVICE

Religion that God our Father accepts as pure and faultless is this: to look after orphans and widows in their distress and to keep oneself from being polluted by the world.

James 1:27

I remember a time when my youth group at church purposefully helped others. We all, as a group, had decided we wanted to focus on James 1:27 during Spring Break, so we did. My youth group went to homes of widows and orphans. We divided into small groups and went to many different homes. Some groups mowed yards, pulled weeds, and helped clean houses. It felt so good ministering to others, it was such hard work, but God kept me going, knowing that I was doing work to glorify Him. I was surprised that one group went to my home and did yard work. My parents had recently traveled to Korea and adopted a baby boy. My dad had not had time to mow the yard. I was so humbled when others ministered to my very own family. Do you know any widows are orphans? How can you minister to them?

by Kaylie

Praises and Prayers

_____

_____

_____

_____

69 ✟ STUMBLING BLOCK

Accept him whose faith is weak, without passing judgment on disputable matter.
Therefore let us stop passing judgment on one another. Instead, make up your mind not to put any stumbling block or obstacle in your brother's way.

Romans 14:1, 13

There were many times I shared my faith with others and people refused to believe that Christianity is the only way. They either didn't believe in any God or thought that all religions should be considered equal. It was hard for me to accept their way of thinking because I know that there is only one way to God and that they are closing their minds to that one way. I can only pray for them and show them respect even though we disagree. God convicted me that if I don't show them respect, don't listen to why they believe what they do, or if I judge them, then I have lost any future opportunities to witness to them and to show them God's love. Without the opportunity to hear God's Word, they will not believe. I encourage you to pray for the people who believe differently from you so you will know how to share God's Word and love for them! Is there someone in your life that you have caused to stumble?

by Rebekah

Praises and Prayers

_____

_____

_____

_____

70 ✞ SHARING YOUR FAITH

Preach the Word; be prepared in season and out of season; correct, rebuke and encourage - with great patience and careful instruction.
1 Peter 3:15

I encourage you to know as much as you can about the Bible. I have met people who don't believe in God, but they have knowledge of the Bible. They ask questions about things that are in the Bible that are tough to answer. Many have an interest in the historical part of the Bible and ask questions that tested my own knowledge of the Bible. Many authors share historical facts that can prove that the Bible is true! Knowing the historical context helps. For example, if you have knowledge of the first century and how tough the Roman empire was on Christians, you can understand how hard it was to be a Christian. One principle is to never get caught by the same question twice. It is a great way for God to design our personal Bible study. I encourage you to take advantage of your church's library, your youth minister and Sunday school teachers. These people can provide studies to help you understand the Bible better. Also, read the commentaries and side notes in your Bible. You will never have all the answers, but do you seek to learn?

by Rebekah

Praises and Prayers

_____

_____

_____

_____

71 ✟ MISSIONS

"Come, follow me," Jesus said, "and I will make you fishers of men."
Matthew 4:19

I believe God has called me to be a missionary, I plan to go to college, but afterwards become a missionary.   I believe there is nothing greater to do in life than serving Jesus. Otherwise, what am I here for? Jesus has called every Christian to go out and to become fishers of men. It may not be missionary work in a foreign country that God has called me to do, but for now, I believe that He has. I will wait on God's timing as I seek His plan for my life.

Fishermen actively pursue fish. Fishermen learn as much as they can about catching fish. They equip themselves with the right gear. They go to the area of the water where fish are located. Are you actively pursuing the lost?   Are you equipped with God's Word to go fishing for the lost?

by Kaylie

Praises and Prayers

_____

_____

_____

_____

72 ☩ HOW SHOULD I LIVE MY LIFE?

However, I consider my life worth nothing to me, if only I may finish the race and complete the task the Lord Jesus has given me - he task of testifying to the gospel of God's grace.

Acts 20:24

God has given you everything you need to be victorious in your life. Do you share your faith openly with others? Have you considered that God has brought people into your life for you to testify to them about God's grace? "Testify" is a fancy word that just means to tell what God has done for you. Witnesses testify in court to what they have seen and heard or experienced. Do others know that God has provided ways to be victorious in the races of life we encounter daily? Do you want anyone to go through life issues or trials without God. Of course not! Our task is to share the saving grace of Jesus with others. Have you shared the gospel of God's grace with anyone today?

Praises and Prayers

---

73 ✞ CAN I BE SEPARATED FROM GOD'S LOVE?

For I am convinced that neither death nor life, neither angels nor demons, neither the present nor the future, nor any powers, neither height nor depth, nor anything else in all creation, will be able to separate us from the love of God that is in Christ Jesus our Lord.
Romans 8:38-39

Have you ever felt lonely and isolated? Have you ever felt you are separated from God and facing battles on your own? The Bible promises that nothing can separate you from God's love. If you have asked Christ to be your Savior and Lord than you can claim this promise! Often, when my daughter is extremely sick with CF and hospitalized, it is easy to feel alone. But, God promises that He is with me. On the way to and from the hospital, I pray. I feel God's presence and I'm overcome with God's love. When are the times you are most challenged and you feel abandoned?   Do you know that God is with you at all times?

by Marilyn

Praises and Prayers

_____

_____

_____

_____

74 ✞ TRUSTING GOD'S PLANS

No eye has seen, no ear has heard, no mind has conceived what God has prepared for those who love him.

1 Corinthians 2:9

We can't even conceive the plans that God has for us. If we pray and read the Bible, God will reveal his plans. One summer, I went to the doctor for a mammogram. The results indicated breast cancer. I was shocked and wondered how this could be God's plan for me! Through this cancer journey I have seen a BIGGER GOD. I had surgery to remove the tumor and six weeks of radiation. Now, I have a new awareness of God's presence in my life! I realized that God is greater than anything and any battle that I will ever encounter. I have a new boldness to share my faith with others. This cancer battle changed my perspective. God has prepared for me a ministry to others with cancer. Are you aware of how much God loves you? When in a difficult situation, do you ask "Why me?" Or, do you depend on God? God uses both the bad things and the good things in life to reveal His presence to you. What does God have prepared for you today?

by Marilyn

Praises and Prayers

_____

_____

_____

_____

75 ✟ GOD WILL MAKE YOUR PATHS STRAIGHT

Trust in the LORD with all your heart and lean not on your own understanding; in all your ways acknowledge him, and he will make your paths straight.

Proverbs 3: 5-6

I just don't understand why this is happening! Have you ever heard that from a friend? Have you ever said it? The Bible promises that we can TRUST the Lord. We don't have to understand the events of today because God sees the big picture of our lives. When facing problems, do you try to figure it out on your own? Do you weigh your understanding of the situation and possibilities that appear logical? The Bible encourages us to trust and acknowledge God. One meaning of "acknowledge" is "to learn to know." We must put our faith in God's love for us and learn to know Him. If we do, we'll get a different perspective. Are you trying to solve your problems today with your limited understanding or are you trusting in God for guidance?

Praises and Prayers

_____

_____

_____

_____

76 ✟ TRUST

You intended to harm me, but God intended it for good to accomplish what is now being done, the saving of many lives.
Genesis 50:20

Joseph's brothers sold him into slavery. Once their father Jacob died, they were afraid that Joseph would take revenge on them. However, Joseph had matured in the Lord to where he saw through circumstances that God's hand was on him. This is the Old Testament equivalent of Romans 8:28, *And we know that in all things God works for the good of those who love him, who have been called according to his purpose.* Do you see God at work through your frustrations? Maybe you don't, but God promises that He is there working things out for good just like He did in Joseph's time. When things seem to be against you, and you know you have done nothing wrong, it is time to learn to trust in the Lord! Start looking for the promises He gives you in the Bible. Will you trust God in difficult situations?

Praises and Prayers

_____

_____

_____

_____

77 ☦ GOD WILL RENEW YOU

Even youths grow tired and weary, and young men stumble and fall; but those who hope in the LORD will renew their strength. They will soar on wings like eagles; they will run and not grow weary, they will walk and not be faint.
Isaiah 40:30-31

Weary! At times, the fatigue is so great that it seems we can't take another step. The physical demands of life are overwhelming at times. Maybe that's when you should evaluate the meetings, clubs, and extra-curricular activities that you participate in on a regular basis. Are they all necessary? It is impossible to be part of all activities at school and at church. Are there any groups or activities that you can eliminate? Can you rearrange your schedule so you can get plenty of rest? Take time to eat healthy foods – don't always choose fast food. God promises to renew your strength. Will you claim that promise?

Praises and Prayers

_____

_____

_____

_____

78 ✞ GOD OF YESTERDAY, TODAY AND TOMORROW

Jesus Christ is the same yesterday, today, and forever.
Hebrews 13:8

I surrendered my heart to Christ to be my Savior and Lord when I was seven years old. When I encounter a difficult situation, I know that the God who saved me many years ago is the same God who is with me today. I understand that since I trusted God for my eternal destination that I can trust God with the problems of today. When I was diagnosed with breast cancer, He made Himself so real to me. God had prepared me for this ordeal because I had seen Him work in my life in countless trials. God will see us through any trial – great or small. Can you trust the God who saved you and gave you eternal life to be the God who is with you today?

by Marilyn

Praises and Prayers

_____

_____

_____

_____

79 ✞ RUNNING THE RACE WITH PURPOSE

Do you not know that in a race all the runners run, but only one gets the prize? Run in such a way as to get the prize. Everyone who competes in the games goes into strict training. They do it to get a crown that will not last; but we do it to get a crown that will last forever.
1 Corinthians 9:24-25

When you are cheering for your team, do you want them to win? Of course! It is more fun to cheer when our team is ahead! To win, each team member needs to be conditioned and trained for the tasks. Football receivers train to run fast and out-maneuver the opponent. Baseball players constantly take batting practice so they can hit the ball precisely. Cheerleaders need to train for endurance to cheer the entire game. We face races in life daily to listen to God and do God's will. What race are you running today? Are you conditioned for life's challenges? We can train for life by reading the Bible and daily applying its principles. Are you trained in God's Word so you can run today's race?

Praises and Prayers

80 ✟ WHAT DO YOU TREASURE?

Do not store up for yourselves treasures on earth, where moth and rust destroy, and where thieves break in and steal. But store up for yourselves treasures in heaven, where moth and rust do not destroy, and where thieves do not break in and steal. For where your treasure is, there your heart will be also.

Matthew 6:19-21

When we treasure something, we take extra precautions to take care of it. My wedding ring is a treasure. I have had it for over forty years and it represents a wedding vow to my husband. When I remove this ring, I put it in a special place for safe keeping. But, my ring can be lost or stolen. Nothing that we own on earth will last forever. How do you put treasures in heaven? The only thing that is going to heaven is people. We must invest our lives in people if we are to put treasures in heaven. If our treasure is in Heaven, it is safe for eternity. Where is your treasure?

by Marilyn

Praises and Prayers

---

81 ✟ HEAVEN IS REAL – SHARE YOUR FAITH

In my Father's house are many rooms; if it were not so, I would have told you. I am going there to prepare a place for you.
John 14:2

Heaven is real! Scripture describes a place for those who have surrendered their lives to Christ as Lord and Savior. God is there and we will spend eternity in His Presence. Do you keep it a secret? Or, do you actively share about the great and mighty things that God has provided? We all will spend eternity in Heaven or Hell, but everyone doesn't understand that Jesus died on the cross for them personally.   Do you know if your loved ones are going to Heaven? Have you shared with others this exciting news? Are you keeping Heaven a secret?

Praises and Prayers

Go Tell

See these lost people – they're all around you.
You may not know them, but I do.

Who are the Lost? They are in the next car,
They're next in line at the store, that's who they are.

Family, strangers, could be your best friend.
They're lost, that's what matters in the end.

But I knew them before they were born.
I know when they're happy, I know when they mourn.

I know their thoughts and words before spoken.
They are lost and my heart is broken.

I love them!

Who will tell them about my love?
Who will tell about my Son from above,

Who came down to earth to save them
From the one prowling for souls to condemn?

Who will be my hands and feet?
Who will be my voice on the street?

I don't want ONE of these to be lost,
For I've paid the ultimate cost.

On a cruel cross, my only begotten Son died,
Eternal life, for believers, will not be denied.

Will you be the one?
Will you tell the lost about my Son?

I know it sounds scary,
But do not tarry.

I'll give you courage and words – all you need to know
For telling the Lost – now please go!

I love them!

© Beth Perry . Used by permission.

82 ✞ HEAVEN

Not everyone who says to me, 'Lord, Lord,' will enter the kingdom of heaven, but only he who does the will of my Father who is in heaven. Many will say to me on that day, 'Lord, Lord, did we not prophesy in your name, and in your name drive out demons and perform many miracles? Then I will tell them plainly, 'I never knew you. Away from me, you evildoers!'
Matthew 7:21-22

My great-grandma, Laura Fry, used to always say how she longed to be with Jesus. I thought that was dumb when I was little; why would someone want to leave this earth? But, now that I am older, I understand what was meant. She had served her time for Jesus, and she was ready to go and be with Him. My great-grandma had such a peace about her, a peace that I couldn't understand. She was so relaxed about everything, she didn't worry about what was going to happen in the days to come. She always said," Don't worry, Jesus will take care of it." I know for sure that my great-grandma went to heaven, she was such a Godly woman. She knew Jesus as her Savior and Lord and was always sharing with us about Him. Do you really know Jesus? Will you enter the kingdom of heaven?

by Kaylie

Praises and Prayers

_____

_____

_____

_____

83 ✝ COMPLETE TASKS

Therefore go and make disciples of all nations, baptizing them in the name of the Father and of the Son and of the Holy Spirit, and teaching them to obey everything I have commanded you. And surely I am with you always, to the very end of the age."

Matthew 28:19-20

Christians have the security of eternity in Heaven. Our sins are forgiven and removed far from us. Why does God leave us here? He could just take us on to heaven when we trust Him, but He has a task for each of us. We have security – the world needs security – our reason for security should be shared. We have the task of testifying about our great and mighty God. Are you sharing the information that can change the eternal destination of your friends and family? What friend can you testify about God's grace today?

Praises and Prayers

_____

_____

_____

_____

84 ✝ LET YOUR LIGHT SHINE FOR JESUS

In the same way, let your light shine before men, that they may see your good deeds and praise your Father in heaven.
Matthew 5:16

A small candle when lit will light up a room. You can even see a small candle in a large, dark auditorium. Have you ever been to a candlelight service where everyone's candle is lit in turn from one small candle? The resulting glow is inspiring. Light makes things visible. We can share the light with others. Our light is a reflection of Jesus Christ. This light shows brightly when we are kind and considerate to others. Basically, it is loving our neighbors as ourselves. Does your light make Jesus more visible to others? What can you do today so that others can see the light of Jesus Christ?

Praises and Prayers

_____

_____

_____

_____

85 ✟ HOW YOU TREAT OTHERS

Do to others as you would have them do to you.
Luke 6:31

My mom is very fun and loves to joke around. She isn't a strict or mean mom. She is Christ-like and loving and is totally against drama. Mom has taught me that I need to treat others as I would have them treat me, and that is really hard sometimes. I always try to remember this Scripture and treat others the way that I want them to treat me! Everyone wants to be treated fairly and with respect. I know that's how I want to be treated. We all want to be treated with kindness. How did you treat your family members today? How do you treat your friends at school?

by Harley

Praises and Prayers

_____

_____

_____

_____

86 ✟ GOD'S PROTECTION

The LORD is my shepherd, I shall not be in want. He makes me lie down in green pastures, he leads me beside quiet waters, he restores my soul. He guides me in paths of righteousness for his name's sake. Even though I walk through the valley of the shadow of death, I will fear no evil, for you are with me; your rod and your staff, they comfort me. You prepare a table before me in the presence of my enemies. You anoint my head with oil; my cup overflows. Surely goodness and love will follow me all the days of my life, and I will dwell in the house of the LORD forever.
Psalms 23

My dad is a firefighter and he gets called for dangerous fires all the time and it worries me sometimes. If it's not done correctly or if something goes wrong anything could happen. When I hear a fire engine siren I think my dad is about to be near a dangerous fire. This Psalm makes me feel safe. Commit it to memory. When you are fearful, will you claim this special Psalm to calm your fears?

by Harley

Praises and Prayers

_____

_____

_____

_____

87 ✞ LOVE FOR GOD

Love the LORD your God with all your heart and with all your soul and with all your strength. These commandments that I give you today are to be upon your hearts. Impress them on your children. Talk about them when you sit at home and when you walk along the road, when you lie down and when you get up.
Deuteronomy 6:5-7

Harley shares: "My Gigi and Papa take Hayden and me to Disneyland every year and we always have a great time! We have so much fun just being together. My grandparents are always there for me. They tell me they pray for Hayden and me every night. Gigi and Papa have taught me that they will love me unconditionally no matter what." Harley's Papa just happens to be my brother, Randy. He and my sister-in-law, Natalie, purposefully seek to impress on the hearts of their young granddaughters the importance of God's commandments. Randy is a successful realtor and he openly shares how God is the focal point of his success. Are God's commandments on your heart? Do you really love the Lord your God with all your heart? Can you share your love for God with children or other teenagers who are in your family?

by Marilyn

Praises and Prayers

_____

_____

_____

_____

88 ✝ SIN TAKEN AWAY

We all, like sheep, have gone astray, each of us has turned to his own way; and the LORD has laid on him the iniquity of us all.
Isaiah 53:6

It is easy for us to identify with the sheep that have gone astray. We can all recall things from our past wherein we have failed. However, for some of us it is much more difficult to believe that Jesus has actually taken those things away. Sometimes we still want to hang on to our guilt, not believing that God really did lay our iniquity onto His Son. Pastor John Meador conducts a special service on Good Friday evening where he builds a huge cross on the stage while he is sharing the story of that day. He chips away at the wood with his hatchet as he assembles a cross. Toward the end of the service assistants help him stand the cross up and secure it for all to see. It is a very moving service. At the close, Pastor Meador invites any who would like to write out their sins on a scrap of paper to come nail them to the cross. It is a very vivid picture of what Jesus has actually done for each of us. Can you see your sins nailed to the cross? Jesus truly has borne them away *as far as the east is from the west.* Have you thanked Him and given Him praise for His great gift of salvation?

Praises and Prayers

_____

_____

_____

_____

89 ✟ STRENGTH

Though one may be overpowered, two can defend themselves. A cord of three strands is not quickly broken.
Ecclesiastes 4:12

Every year, I go to the Susan G. Komen *Race for the Cure*. You pay money to register and you can enter a race or walk for cancer. The money you give goes to research that helps find a cure for cancer. I have entered the *Race for the Cure* for six years. All of the women on my mom's side of the family participate. There are four generations that participate: my great-grandmother, my grandmother, my mom, and my little sister and me. My great grandmother has been a breast cancer survivor for many years. Treatments are much better now than they were years ago. Raising money at the race will help find even better treatment and hopefully a cure. My great-grandmother surviving such a terrible disease helps me realize that you can overcome anything as long as you surrender it to God and trust Him. He will never give you any problem you can't handle. The support that my family has for each other will never be broken. How can you support friends through trials? Can you stand united with others in prayer?

by Harley

Praises and Prayers

_____

_____

_____

_____

90 ✝ OVERCOMING FEAR

In God, whose word I praise, in the LORD, whose word I praise - in God I trust; I will not be afraid. What can man do to me?

Psalms 56: 10-11

I was very busy during high school with homework, friends, being a cheerleader and having to deal with many hours every day administering breathing treatments. Sometimes, I felt I never really belonged in a group with my healthy friends because they never understood what I had to deal with on a daily basis. My friends never fully grasped my battle with medical situations. This made me feel lonely and I felt afraid that I will never belong anywhere. The only way I felt connected to someone was when that person had another disease. When I read this Psalm, I decided not to be afraid of what others think. I should just focus on what God thinks. God is the only who has given me joy and has given me confidence. What fears have you been holding on to? Have you let God take away your fears?

by Rebekah

Praises and Prayers

_____

_____

_____

_____

91 ☩ CHOICES

Yet, O LORD, you are our Father. We are the clay, you are the potter; we are all the work of your hand.

Isaiah 64:8

As a teenager, I did not choose to trust God's wisdom concerning the many adjustments I had to make. I grew up resentful that my parents had moved me nineteen times before I finished high school. But one day when I was an adult, God spoke to me as I was waiting to teach a Bible study to a group of ladies. As I looked around the room I realized I knew the personal story of every lady there. God spoke: "See how I used the adjustments you had to make to prepare you to minister to all kinds of people?" Choose to trust Him and He will shape your life to fit His purpose and bring you great joy. Will you trust Him today?

by Barbara

Praises and Prayers

_____

_____

_____

_____

92 ✞ LOVING OTHERS

A friend loves at all times.
Proverbs 17:17a

Every year at my school, the Seniors went on a traditional week-long trip in March to the place of their choice. My class voted to go to Disney World. We were so excited about making final memories of fun before we went our separate ways after graduating. About a month before the trip, I expressed my concern to some close friends about my medical needs. I required someone to do chest physical therapy on my lungs daily so I could breathe. This meant I had to bring one of my parents along with me. I was torn between two things - making my final fun memories with friends, or staying separately with a parent taking care of my medical needs. I wanted time with my friends with NO parental supervision. I was tempted not to go on this trip. I was frustrated that CF was going to stop me from having fun! My mom told me that my friends offered to learn how to do the therapy so I could go with them on the trip without a parent coming along. At school one day, my friends learned how to do the therapy. Mom taught them how to "clap" on my lungs. They admitted that they were nervous doing it. I helped my friends by telling them to do the clapping harder or softer. My friends did a very good job during the Senior trip! I had so much fun! What are ways you can show that you love your friends?

by Rebekah

Praises and Prayers

_____

_____

_____

_____

93 ✟ NOTHING IS TOO HARD FOR GOD

I am the LORD, the God of all mankind. Is anything too hard for me?
Jeremiah 32:27

Often when in a difficult situation, we tend to think that God just isn't big enough for the tasks and doesn't even know what is going on in our life. For instance, when I was looking for a job to return to teaching at age fifty, I thought that God had simply forgotten about me. Maybe it was just too difficult for God to provide a job for a fifty year-old woman. I went to numerous interviews but the competition was great and it seemed like younger applicants were always chosen. A friend, Linda Whitten, asked her principal to interview me. The interview went great and, I was hired to teach second grade. This principal, Mike Dukes, was a former pastor. Years later, when I had breast cancer, God used this Christian principal to encourage my heart and he prayed for me. Mike made sure my class was covered while I left early to go to radiation treatments. God didn't just have a job, God had the perfect job for me, I just had to be patient! God is so great and so mighty. Are you facing a difficult situation? Is there anything too hard for God?

by Marilyn

Praises and Prayers

_____

_____

_____

_____

94 ✞ WHOM DO YOU SERVE?

Whatever you do, work at it with all your heart, as working for the Lord, not for men, since you know that you will receive an inheritance from the Lord as a reward. It is the Lord Christ you are serving.
Colossians 3:23-24

When we are at work, we try extra hard to please our boss. Our boss is in control of our paycheck and could determine how long we are employed. We want to be rewarded. If the boss is in the same room, we try even harder to good job. So, how hard should we try when we are doing God's work? Scriptures say that we should work with all of our heart in whatever we do. Would that include Bible studies or homework projects? Should you always do you best when you are helping in Vacation Bible school or at youth camp? You won't get a physical paycheck, but your account is eternal. Your reward is in Heaven. Are you doing all tasks as if Christ is in the room with you?

Praises and Prayers

_____

_____

_____

_____

95 ✝ GOD STRENGTHENS YOU

For the eyes of the LORD range throughout the earth to strengthen those whose hearts are fully committed to him.

2 Chronicles 16:9a

Often, we are overcommitted with activities due to time restraints! We can only do so much in 24 hours each day. Doing homework and making good grades, developing friendships, being involved in church activities and cheerleading are what consumes the life of many students. What is difficult is the fact that all of the activities are good things. Are you committed to making good grades enough to sacrifice the time required? Is your heart really in it? God looks for our "heart attitude" to determine if we are committed to doing His will. It's harder than it sounds. Being committed to God means that we are willing to invest the time necessary to accomplish God's will. It takes time to read the Bible and pray. Is your heart fully committed to doing God's will?

Praises and Prayers

_____

_____

_____

_____

96 ✞ GOD CHOSE YOU

You did not choose me, but I chose you and appointed you to go and bear fruit — fruit that will last. Then the Father will give you whatever you ask in my name.

John 15:16

Adopted children are chosen. My niece, Valerie, and her husband, James, just spent one and half years in the adoption process. They traveled to Korea from Texas to get their baby boy, Seth! He's part of our family now. Seth will always know that his parents went to great lengths to get him. He was chosen! Did you know that God chose you to be His child? You are adopted into His family. God not only chose you but has a purpose for you to bear fruit. By sharing your faith, God will use you to bring others to the saving grace of Jesus Christ. What kind of fruit are you bearing today?

by Marilyn

Praises and Prayers

_____

_____

_____

_____

97 ✛ POWER AVAILABLE TO CHRISTIANS

When you pass through the waters, I will be with you; and when you pass through the rivers, they will not sweep over you. When you walk through the fire, you will not be burned; the flames will not set you ablaze. For I am the Lord, your God, the Holy One of Israel, your Savior.
Isaiah 43:2-3a

Regardless of what we go through, when we belong to God we have His promises and need not be overwhelmed nor defeated. He will sustain us. We may find ourselves misjudged, lied about, and mistreated in many ways. But we have a secret weapon that gives us the inner power to overcome – faith in the God of this universe who is our Strength, our Guide and Lover of Our Souls. We all go "through" hard times, but He is with us every step of the way and eventually takes us to the other side of our circumstances. And when we arrive there, we find ourselves changed, stronger in our faith and filled with the peace of God. Do you realize that God is your "secret weapon" and available to you today?

by Barbara

Praises and Prayers

---

98 ✝ LIVE A WORTHY LIFE

As a prisoner for the Lord, then, I urge you to live a life worthy of the calling you have received. Be completely humble and gentle; be patient, bearing with one another in love.
Ephesians 4:1-2

A prisoner has no choices. If in jail, prisoners must follow the rules. They get up, get dressed, eat and go to bed following the authority of the system. Are you following God's authority? Are you living a life that is worthy of the calling that you received from our Lord and Savior? So what would that life look like? The Bible describes it as a life filled with humility and gentleness and bearing one another in love. Humility comes to as we see the greatness and glory of God and we are overwhelmed by our own weakness and sinfulness. Gentleness is the very character of Christ. We are patient with others as God is patient with us. God's love flowing through us is what makes all of the other qualities work. Do you bear one another in love? How are you showing love to others?

Praises and Prayers

_____

_____

_____

_____

99 ✝ FEARS

***I sought the LORD, and he answered me; he
delivered me from all my fears.***
Psalms 34:4

In 1998, I was diagnosed with Cystic Fibrosis Related Diabetes (CFRD). Having two diseases is an extremely hard crusade. I have many hours of breathing treatments. I was scared because I knew that I had to make decisions that best fit my disease. I became more organized with my choices. For example, I cannot go out to dinner after seven o'clock. This is especially true during the weekends because the restaurant is crowded and it takes longer to get food, then my blood sugar drops too low. I always can have a snack but my appetite decreases and I can't enjoy dinner. Also, I can't stay out too late because I have to do my breathing treatments on a regular schedule which leaves me exhausted the next day. I was afraid of having another disease and additional responsibility. But I was comforted by this Scripture which reminded me to give all my fears to God. God will take my burden! I gave this new health issue to God. Do you understand that your choices today affect your future? What fears are you facing? Do you realize that God will deliver you from your fears?

by Rebekah

Praises and Prayers

_____

_____

_____

_____

100 ✞ MARCHING ORDERS

Forget the former things; do not dwell on the past. See, I am doing a new thing! Now it springs up; do you not perceive it? I am making a way in the desert and streams in the wasteland.
Isaiah 43:18-19

Thank God for new beginnings! Every day offers a new start, an opportunity to choose to grow, to serve and to become more and more like Jesus. As long as we look back, whether it be at successes or failures, we cannot move forward in dependence upon the Lord as we should. Leave the past behind and look at God afresh each morning! Our first waking words should be, "Good morning, Lord. What are my marching orders for today? I am at your service." When we surrender to His plan, He reveals Himself to others through our lives and we experience the joy of the Lord. Are you ready for your marching orders from God for today?

by Barbara

Praises and Prayers

_____

_____

_____

_____

101 ☩ ARE YOU READY

Then I heard the voice of the Lord saying, "Whom shall I send? And who will go for us?" And I said, "Here am I. Send me!"
Isaiah 6:8

Have you been preparing for life after high school? Have you thought about where you will spend your time and effort when cheerleading practices and football games are over? There will be a time when you follow your dreams for you future. What do your dreams include? Are you planning on college and a career? Do your plans include seeking and doing God's will for your life? God saved you to share your faith with others. The only things going to Heaven are people. Are you ready to go where God sends you? When you hear God's calling for your life, what is your response?

Praises and Prayers

_____

_____

_____

_____

Scripture Index

OLD TESTAMENT

Book	Verses	Devotion
Genesis	50:20	76
Exodus	14:14	13
Exodus	20:12	88
Deuteronomy	6:5-7	87
1 Kings	19:12	16
2 Chronicles	6:19	95
Psalms	23	86
Psalms	31:4	91
Psalms	33:22	14
Psalms	34:4	99
Psalms	46:10	16
Psalms	56:10-11	90
Psalms	71:14	23
Psalms	103:13	3
Psalms	119:11	40
Psalms	119:27	41
Psalms	119:35	53
Psalms	139:12	1
Proverbs	3:5-6	75
Proverbs	4:23	39
Proverbs	17:17	92
Proverbs	22:6	63
Proverbs	27:19	28

Book	Verses	Devotion
Proverbs	29:2	60
Proverbs	29:4	60
Proverbs	31:13-17	62
Proverbs	31:25-29	60
Proverbs	31:30	61
Ecclesiastes	4:12	89
Isaiah	6:8	101
Isaiah	40:30-31	77
Isaiah	43:2-3	97
Isaiah	43:18-19	100
Isaiah	49:16	9
Isaiah	53:6	88
Isaiah	64:8	91
Jeremiah	23:29	53
Jeremiah	29:11	65
Jeremiah	32:27	93

NEW TESTAMENT

Book	Verses	Devotion
Matthew	4:19	71
Matthew	5:10	15
Matthew	5:16	84
Matthew	6:19-21	80
Matthew	6:34	52
Matthew	7:21-22	82

Book	Verses	Devotion
Matthew	7:23	25
Matthew	7:24-25	56
Matthew	12:35	39
Matthew	17:20	33
Matthew	18:6	58
Matthew	18:19-20	36
Matthew	19:13-14	33
Matthew	28:19-20	83
Matthew	28:20	9
Luke	11:34	8
Mark	10:13-16	6
Luke	6:31	85
Luke	19:17	64
John	3:16	25
John	4:1-26	31
John	6:31	85
John	13:7	43
John	13:34-35	27
John	14:2	81
John	15:16	96
John	17	81
Acts	20:24	72
Romans	3:23	2
Romans	8:28	18, 76
Romans	8:38-39	73
Romans	12:12	37, 54

Book	Verses	Devotion
Romans	14:1, 13	69
Romans	15:13	11
1 Corinthians	2:9	74
1 Corinthians	3:16	55
1 Corinthians	6:18	19
1 Corinthians	9:24-25	79
1 Corinthians	10:13	19
1 Corinthians	14:33	7, 29
1 Corinthians	15:33	57
2 Corinthians	1:3-4	12
Galatians	5:22-26	26
Galatians	5:22	27-33
Galatians	5:22-23	34, 35
Ephesians	1:5	24
Ephesians	2:8-9	4
Ephesians	2:10	5, 64
Ephesians	3:20	10, 20
Ephesians	4:1-2	98
Ephesians	4:17, 22-23	44
Ephesians	4:22-24	45
Ephesians	4:29, 32	46
Ephesians	5:1-2	47
Ephesians	5:3-4	48
Ephesians	5:6-8	49
Ephesians	5:15-17	50

Book	Verses	Devotion
Ephesians	5:20	51
Ephesians	6:11-12	22
Ephesians	6:17	17
Colossians	3:23-24	94
Philippians	2:14	54
Philippians	4:7	8
Philippians	4:13	59
Philippians	4:19	21
1 Thessalonians	5:16-18	38
Hebrews	12:2	38
Hebrews	13:8	65, 78
James	1:2-4	54
James	1:20	35
James	1:27	68
James	2:14-17	52
James	2:18, 26	67
James	3:1-2	35
James	5:7	30
James	5:16	42
1 Peter	3:15	70
1 Peter	3:15-16	66

ABOUT MARILYN PHILLIPS

Marilyn Phillips is a Cum Laude graduate of Texas Woman's University. She taught second grade students for eighteen years. Marilyn was a cheerleader coach at Temple Christian School. She is a breast cancer survivor and praises God for the journey! Marilyn enjoys writing and praises God for her success. Articles have been published in national magazine publications including *Guideposts, Obadiah, Home Life, Parent Life,* and *Living with Teenagers.*

Six students helped Marilyn write the book, *Fort Worth Kids' View.* Authors were interviewed on TV affiliates of ABC, NBC, CBS and FOX. They also received a letter from President George W. Bush and First Lady Laura Bush. Authors also received letters from 30 state governors.

Eight book contributions include *Chicken Soup for the Soul: Tales of Christmas, Chicken Soup for the Soul: True Love, Chicken Soup for the Soul: Christmas, Living By Faith, God Allows U-Turns: American Moments, God Allows U-Turns, Extraordinary Kids,* and *Chicken Soup for the Surviving Soul.*

She has six published books including: *Called from the Dust: A Journey of Faith, Hope and Love* (co-written with Elizabeth "Moi" Lalnunmawi), *Cheering for Eternity, God Speaks to Cheerleaders, A Cheerleader for Life, Fort Worth Kids' View* and *PRINCESS.*

Marilyn has been married to her husband, Nolan, since 1972. He is a graduate of Texas Tech and an engineer. Nolan has taught adult Bible study classes for over 40 years. They live in Bedford, Texas, and have two grown children, Bryant and Rebekah.

For more information, visit Marilyn's webpage at www.mphillipsauthor.com.

ABOUT REBEKAH PHILLIPS

Rebekah Phillips was a high school cheerleader for two years at Temple Christian School. Her team won 1st place at Christian Cheerleaders of America (CCA) Camps both years. She was also co-captain of the dancing drill team.

Rebekah's life is a tremendous testimony to her faith in God. She was the guest speaker at the CCA National Competition in Chattanooga, Tennessee. After Rebekah gave her testimony sharing how God has helped her dealing with Cystic Fibrosis, she received a standing ovation from over 450 cheerleaders who were there to compete. Rebekah gained national recognition when she was chosen from high school cheerleaders across the nation to receive the prestigious *Rianne Ellisa Scrivner Christian Cheerleader Courage Award* for displaying outstanding courage in the face of extraordinary trials. Rebekah is vivacious and truly incredible.

Rebekah has Cystic Fibrosis. Doctors said that she would only live until age 13. Medical research, dedicated doctors, and the power of prayer have helped Rebekah achieve her life-long dream of graduating from college and becoming a teacher. Rebekah is a 2002 graduate of University of North Texas.

Rebekah is an avid reader and enjoys writing. Marilyn and Rebekah co-authored a children's book, *PRINCESS,* about a little girl who has cystic fibrosis. She has an article published in *Chicken Soup for the Soul: Tough Time, Tough People*. Rebekah's latest book is *A Breath with God: My battle with Cystic Fibrosis*. This book has over 50 Scripture references and encourages anyone with diseases to focus on God. This book is available at www.mphillipsauthor.com.

CONTRIBUTORS

Harley Teel is in middle school at Fort Worth Christian School. Harley enjoys tumbling and cheerleading. She volunteers with pre-school children at her church and is an excellent role model for them. Harley is a honor roll student and competes in academic meets every year. Brad and Brooke are her parents. Harley has a younger sister named Hayden

Kaylie McDuff is a high school student and enjoys soccer, playing the guitar and ukulele, and, when time allows, writing. Kaylie also loves to hang out with her youth group at church and study the Word of God. Kaylie has two younger sisters and a brother. James and Valerie are her parents. After graduation, Kaylie plans to attend college.

Beth Perry is a freelance writer living in Ft. Worth, Texas with her husband, Ken. They have four children and four grandchildren in the Dallas/Ft. Worth area. Beth has been an executive assistant in the corporate world and is now taking time to reflect on the incredible ways God has been in and through her life.

Barbara Christa is a gifted Bible teacher. She has a Bachelor's Degree in Elementary Education from Southwest Texas University and a Master's in Education from the University of Houston. Barbara has been a church staff member for over 27 years in various capacities. She is on staff at North Richland Hills Baptist Church as Interim Minister of Single Adults. Barbara is married to David and they have one daughter.

HOW TO RECEIVE CHRIST

The Romans Road is a way of explaining the good news of salvation using only verses from the Book of Romans.

1) Acknowledge that you are a sinner.
    Romans 3:23 *For all have sinned and fall short of the glory of God.*
2) Know that all sin leads to death.
    Romans 6:23 *For the wages of sin is death, but the gift of God is eternal life in Christ Jesus our Lord.*
3) Know that there is hope through a Savior!
    Romans 6:23b *But the gift of God is eternal life through Jesus Christ our Lord.* Romans 5:8 *But God demonstrates his own love for us in this: While we were still sinners, Christ died for us.*
4) Confess your sins to God.
    Romans 10:9 *That if you confess with your mouth, "Jesus is Lord," and believe in your heart that God raised him from the dead, you will be saved.* Romans 10:13 *For, "Everyone who calls on the name of the Lord will be saved."*
5) Have a relationship with God.
    Romans 5:1 *Therefore, since we have been justified through faith, we have peace with God through our Lord Jesus Christ.*
6) Realize God's promise
    Romans 8:38-39 *For I am convinced that neither death nor life, neither angels nor demons, neither the present nor the future, nor any powers, neither height nor depth, nor anything else in all creation, will be able to separate us from the love of God that is in Christ Jesus our Lord.*
7) Say a simple prayer to God acknowledging your sin and that you deserve the punishment of death, state that you believe that Jesus came and took the death penalty for your sins, and because of your faith in God you know that you can be saved and forgiven and that you place your trust in Jesus Christ.

If you have made a decision to ask Jesus Christ into your life

OR

If you have questions about receiving Christ or about the ministry of CCA

Please contact us

TOLL FREE at: 1.877.CHEERCCA

E-Mail us at: info@cheercca.com

Write to us at:

CCA

P O Box 49

Bethania, NC 27010

GOD LOVES YOU!!

A Breath with God: My Battle with Cystic Fibrosis

Rebekah's faith in God has given her hope and strength to fight this life threatening disease. Many have said this book was an encouragement in fighting the battles of life. Rebekah shares how the Word of God challenged her to never give up. There are over 50 Scriptures to encourage and give hope.

Called from the Dust: A Journey of Faith, Hope and Love

This true life story describes how Almighty God led Thang and Moi on a journey of faith into a ministry to India. God put an uneducated jungle boy on a different path. He now has a doctoral degree from Southwestern Baptist Theological Seminary in Fort Worth, Texas. He preaches to the lost and teaches lay pastors in India how to preach the Word of God.

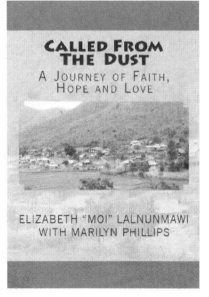

Books available at www.mphillipsauthor.com

Made in the USA
Columbia, SC
22 September 2021